LIGHT FROM A DARK STAR

Where's God when my world falls apart?

by Wayne Kirkland

Scripture Union

Scripture Union, 207–209 Queensway, Bletchley, MK2 2EB, England.

Email:info@scriptureunion.org.uk
Internet:http://www.scriptureunion.org.uk

First published 2001
ISBN 1 85999 515 2

Scripture taken from *The Contemporary English Version*, © 1997
British and Foreign Bible Society; *The Message* © by Eugene H
Peterson, 1993, 1994, 1995, used by permission of NavPress
Publishing Group.

British Library Cataloguing-in-Publication Data
A catalogue record for this book is available from the British Library.

Cover design by Phil Jones of Waldon White Jones, Essex.
Internal design and typesetting by Sue Jackson.

Printed and bound in Great Britain by Creative Print and Design
(Wales) Ebbw Vale.

Light from a dark star

 dark star: starlike object which emits little or no visible light but is known to exist from other evidence

About the author

Name: Wayne Kirkland
Nationality: New Zealander
Married to: Jill
Children: three daughters
Employment: part-time car dealer and part-time writer/administrator with Signpost Communications
Involved in: local school board; several community initiatives; foster care
Lives in: Naenae – a suburb of Greater Wellington, New Zealand
Likes: the quiet of early mornings; picturesque walks; good company; All Black wins
Dislikes: rampant consumerism; fishing and gardening; All Black losses
Most important to me: my faith in God; family and friendships (in a world that seems too busy for them); making a difference
Favourite characters in history: St Patrick; Francis of Assisi; William Wilberforce and Te Whiti
Best movies: *Schindler's List*; *Dead Man Walking*; *The Truman Show*; *Cool Runnings*
Most moving experiences: the births of our children; seeing *Les Miserables*; visiting the Philippines

Contents

Dear readers

Christians write many books on suffering: they are better placed than anyone else, because they believe in a suffering God. But no Christian (or anyone else for that matter) claims to have plumbed the mystery of suffering to its depths. Certainly Wayne Kirkland does not make that claim. But he is well qualified to add to the literature on the subject. His brother and cousin both committed suicide within the space of six months. Imagine the anguish of that!

Of the many books on suffering I have read, this is the most accessible. Wayne faces all the problems head on and sets them out in sharp relief. His style is fast moving and readable, and between the lines I can recognise the gifted Kiwi youth worker to whom I had the privilege of lecturing as he completed postgraduate studies in Vancouver. The book is packed with stories, and this makes it very contemporary, for in our postmodern world the story wins every time over the solid philosophical argument. People can identify with it. They can feel their way into the story – especially when Wayne tells it. I believe this is a very helpful book. Readers may not know Wayne Kirkland – after all he lives half a world away. But they will know him well once they have read this short but immensely appealing book.

Michael Green
Senior Research Fellow at Wycliffe Hall, Oxford, and Adviser in Evangelism to the Archbishops of Canterbury and York

Light from a Dark Star

To my parents Bob and Shirley,
who've kept aglow the light of their own faith in
God in the face of suffering;

and to my wife Jill, who has shared the journey
of my own pain.

And with grateful thanks to Ian Dunwoodie
for his expert assistance in developing the book.

★ ★ ★

1: My diary of pain

Thursday 1:00am

The phone rings – that distant, insistent jangle that drags me from deep sleep. 'It must be some ungodly hour,' I think to myself as I stumble through to the study, ready to give the caller a piece of my mind. I look at the clock. It's 1:00am.

The voice is instantly familiar. 'It's Dad here, Wayne. Sorry to ring you at this time of the night... but I have some very, very bad news. I don't know how to tell you this... Your brother... it's Phil... he's killed himself.'

Quick as that. The words only take a few seconds. My life is never going to be the same again.

The news starts to sink in. Not just shock – sheer panic and terror! Like a knife to my heart. I find myself struggling for breath. My wife Jill is at my side in the study by this time, asking in a frightened voice what's wrong. As I stammer my bewildered questions to Dad she must be gaining some idea.

The rest of the call is brief. I get off the phone, tell Jill and burst into tears. I don't know what to do. I walk downstairs, gasping as I try to take it all in. Cries come from the pit of my stomach – deep, shuddering sobs.

I know instinctively that this is going to be a very long night. Jill rings good friends and they offer to come immediately.

People? People coming? My first thought is to shower and dress!

It's a knee-jerk reaction, but it does help. I need to do something physical, just to cope with the horror of it all. And it also gives me a few minutes by myself. My sobbing doesn't stop in the shower. Painful convulsions of horror and disbelief.

Thursday 4:30am

Over 200 miles to our home town. In his typical fatherly fashion Dad said not to do anything until the morning, but that's a forlorn hope! For an hour I function on 'auto pilot' while Jill and I pack everything we need and load the car. Then, when it's all ready, we wake our three children and tell them what has happened. Within minutes we're in the car, on our way.

Jill tells me to let her know when I want her to take the wheel, but driving keeps my mind active. As we come closer to New Plymouth I think about what we'll find. I feel like turning and driving away, but I know I can't.

Thursday 8:30am

A beautiful, fine, summer morning – and no way of enjoying it. We open the front gate, walk up the path and round to the back of the house. There we peer through the French doors. Someone sees us and unfastens the lock. Inside it's like a battlefield. Bodies on the floor, slumped on chairs... dazed and silent.

Phil's wife, Jo, has just told her three children that their Daddy is dead.

Friday

Waking up brings an avalanche of dreadful feelings. Another warm, sunny morning but I can't celebrate it. Everyone else is the same. Mum and Dad have been up since 4am, talking and crying together, going back over Phil's life.

I walk out onto the back porch. I sit down with Mum and Jill to read the death notices in the morning paper. That simple act brings perhaps the saddest moment I have ever experienced.

There in black and white – the bald statement that my kid brother is dead. This is the end. Utter desolation. We weep and weep.

Saturday

The day of the funeral. We've been preparing ourselves for this moment for two days now. I wish I could attend the service without having to meet anyone, but I know I have to face people. The church is packed to overflowing. Friends have come from everywhere.

The service is a blur, except for a stunning poem by Craig – Phil's business partner: *Phil, you flamed our lives with golden laughter...*

The walk behind the coffin seems a million miles. Everyone is shattered and distraught. Questions. Endless questions.

And so few answers...

Wednesday – one week later

Cricket at the park is soothing – yet another chance to think. But always I come back to the reality that this time last week Phil was alive. Alive and in pain. I wish again and again that I could go back to that week. That I could be with him and talk to him and stop him from doing such an awful thing.

Dinner with family, but I'm bad company. During the meal I keep watching the clock and thinking of each step in the chain of events, the final countdown that's revealed by the phone record:

5:45pm: last inward fax.

5:55pm: returned fax.

6:15–6:30pm: last incoming phone call.

That's all we have to go on. Phil was probably dead by 7pm.

It's quarter to seven now.

I can't take it any longer. I leave, driving to Phil's place of work. Here's where he hanged himself, not to be found for several hours. I walk round the building and think, 'Oh Phil, if only I'd known, if only I was there'.

Suicide seems to make our grieving so much more complicated. If Phil had died in a genuine accident, we could have coped better. Knowing he was in peace, we would only have our own grief and sense of loss to bear... not that untouchable ocean of despair which must have been his. Everything is clouded by the knowledge that this was a conscious choice, the result of Phil's inward hurt and unhappiness.

And we weren't there. He died by himself. No one to witness it. No one to mourn. That's painful. That's excruciatingly painful.

Finally I say my goodbyes, as if it's last week, then drive back along country roads, trying to make sense of it all.

It seemed as bad as it could be, but it wasn't. I think suffering must feed on suffering.

In the months after Phil's death the cloud of despair that wrapped itself around me started to clear a little. Life was beginning to return to some sense of normality. I was looking ahead for the first time with real hope.

And then this...

Sunday night, almost six months later
An exhausting day. Getting close to bedtime and we've been out, so I decide to check the answerphone messages. There's one from Dad. His voice sounds awfully wavery – like something's seriously wrong. He wants me to call him. I do, straight away.

Dad answers and when he discovers who it is he says, 'I've got some more bad news, Wayne. Your cousin Mark has done the same thing as Phil. They found him last night.'

Stunned is not a strong enough word to describe my emotions. I'm overwhelmed with the sense that I have lived through this moment before. I can't believe it. What's happening? Is our family coming apart at the seams?

Wednesday morning, 11:30am

We arrive in the small town where my cousin lived with his family. It's been a long journey – this one even more cruel than the last.

We meet Mum and Dad for lunch in the main street. Still a couple of hours before the funeral. We begin to talk. I can see the pain in their eyes. Actually, it's more than pain. It's fear. They don't speak about it, but it's there. Are either of their remaining sons going to take the same option?

I voice the reassurance they so desperately need to hear. I have no intention of leaving them to deal with even more loss and pain. It's not an option. Never will be.

The relief streams back into their faces and we try to cope with this new grief together.

Wednesday, a week later

Life goes on... and yet the questions still remain. Why? Why? Why?

* * *

2: A planet in pain

 The truth of the matter is that all we have to do is live long enough and we will suffer.

Don Carson

We live in a hurting world. If you've managed to avoid tragedy this far, you're in the minority. From the ease of our comfortable suburbs, the pain may seem distant. We may even for a time deny that life is generally difficult – in fact, grindingly difficult – for most of the six billion inhabitants of Planet Earth. But the truth is, despite the huge advances our civilisation has made, existence for vast numbers of people is more often brutish than civilised, more filled with despair, agony and suffering than it is with hope, joy and fulfilment.

Of course, it's easy to be seduced into thinking that extreme suffering only happens in someone else's backyard, far removed from our own slice of heaven. Easy, that is, until we're confronted with it face-on; until it happens to a friend, family member, neighbour or workmate. It may be incurable cancer, a road death, a tragic accident; a pain-filled disease...

And how many go through suffering-by-association as they watch a loved one waste away with Alzheimer's or MS or AIDS?

To live is to suffer – one of life's primal lessons. None of us escapes it. None of us is a stranger to pain. I'm certainly not. So far I've been spared the physical hurts and disabilities that some people endure but, like everyone else, I've gone through times of misery that have scarred my soul.

We all do. And nobody knows why!

We grow up with suffering. It's part of the world we belong to, and we take it for granted. Until one day the awfulness hits us... and then the questions burst out.

★ Where does suffering come from?

★ Who causes it?

★ How come some people suffer far more than others, more than they ever deserve?

★ Why can't we have a world without all this anguish and heartache?

You've chosen to pick up this book. You've been interested enough to read it this far as I've re-lived my own little chunk of misery. I guess that means *you* wonder about this whole thing, too. Maybe you have the same questions I do? Maybe you're like a number of people I've met. When they hear that I take seriously my faith in God, they buttonhole me and abuse me (mostly in a friendly way!), complaining about what God has done or failed to do in their own lives. Or just generally sounding off about this messy world...

'If God is a God of love... '

'If God is a God of love,' they say, 'how come he lets all this cruelty happen? Why does he allow vicious dictators to brutalise innocent people and turn whole countries into deserts? How can God watch innocent children suffer from earthquakes... or floods... or wars... or lousy parents... or paedophiles... ? Hey, if I was God I'd be ashamed of the way I ran this world... '

Ouch.

Yes, I know the problems only too well. So let me say, right at the beginning: *I cannot make complete sense of human suffering*. This book will not finish with a brilliant explanation of why it exists, and what it's all about, and what God is up to. *I do not fully understand* how he can do nothing when vicious cruelty is carried out by one human against another. Especially when it's a helpless child on the receiving end.

It usually doesn't help when I tell my accusing friends that I ask exactly the same questions they do. Why *does* God allow it? What is wrong with the world? Why doesn't he change it? How can he – if he really loves us – stand back and let happen the things that do happen?

Not everyone who asks me these questions is serious about them. Often all they want is a chance to poke holes in what they see as 'religion'. And that's okay. I don't see myself as being put in this world to defend God. He's big enough to look after himself.

But I can't believe that it's just a case of making God into the Bad Guy. I've known him (in my slow and hesitant way) long enough to be convinced that he's nobody's fool. The more I've discovered about him, the more sure I am that he doesn't do things lightly. And even if this whole problem of pain and suffering doesn't make too much sense to me, I suspect there's more to it than meets the eye.

That's why I don't have any qualms about asking all the tough questions. In fact, I *want* to ask those tough questions. For my own sake as much as yours or anybody else's. And if you're willing to chew them over with me, there's nothing I'd like more.

Something has drawn you to read this book... and it may be the very thing that has driven me to write it. But I can't help thinking I may be stupid even to try it. Suffering? Misery? Pain? Could there be a less promising subject? Especially now, at the beginning of a new millennium. Isn't it time to put the shambles of the past behind us? To launch out into a more promising future? Isn't it time to celebrate the successes of our human potential?

And yet, just as the last millennium ended with the gruesomeness of Kosovo, so the new one is beginning with its own bouts of misery. I'm neither a prophet nor the son of a prophet, but I'll bet my life on one thing – that this promising new millennium will be full of the news of the next viciousness one bunch of humans launches onto another. And the next. It's as if we're locked into some sort of cosmic concentration camp, and the commandant spends his time dreaming up new tortures.

So if you're prepared to read on, to puzzle out these problems along with me, and maybe even to get in touch afterwards and say 'Exactly right' or 'Yeah, but… ', well, I'd appreciate that, and I'd enjoy mulling it all over with you.

Okay?

Right. Now let's get specific. Let's pin God down with a few of his 'mistakes'. After all, if *he's* not responsible for earthquakes, tornadoes, diseases and epidemics, then who is? Just for the record, here's a snapshot of some disasters of the last few decades that he's allowed to wander loose in this world of his. This is my very personal selection of the world's tragedies. Unless stated otherwise, my facts can be verified from *Compton's Interactive Encylopedia* of 1996 (www.comptons. com), but you could easily compile your own grim list from reference books in the medical and history sections of your local library or browsing the Internet. It's a sobering way to spend a couple of hours.

Natural disasters: earthquakes, floods etc

★ **Earthquakes** are a regular phenomenon, dealing death and destruction throughout our planet, and accounting for about 10,000 deaths on average every year. In recent years, Guatemala, Peru, India, Armenia, Iran and Turkey have all experienced quakes killing more than 20,000 people.

★ China was the scene of a major **earthquake** in 1976 which killed nearly a quarter of a million people.

★ In Pakistan in 1992 many **rivers flooded**, causing landslides which resulted in 2000 deaths and 3.2 million people becoming homeless.

★ A 230 kph **cyclone** caused massive devastation in Bangladesh on 30 April 1991, bringing huge **floods**. 150,000 people are estimated to have lost their lives.

Diseases

★ **Arthritis** afflicts 43 million Americans and more millions around the world. This highly debilitating disease affects people in all age groups, including children. (Check out the Arthritis Foundation's web page www.arthritis.org, for example.)

★ Three million people worldwide are thought to have **multiple sclerosis**. Most sufferers are diagnosed between the ages of 30 and 50, reducing their lifespan by 25 per cent on average. (The National Multiple Sclerosis Society has a website at www.nmss.org)

★ **Leprosy** (Hansen's Disease) is one of the most feared diseases of all time. Five and a half million people suffer from it, according to a WHO study of the early nineties. It can be devastating because it attacks the nerves, killing the sense of feeling; many are left with deformed limbs and some go blind.

★ **Alzheimer's Disease** progressively attacks the brain and results in impaired memory, thinking and behaviour. It's estimated that around five or six per cent of elderly people (defined as 65 years plus) are affected by Alzheimer's or some other form of dementia. (See, for example, *Facts about Alzheimer's Disease* at www.cyber-north.com/public or www.alzheimers.org.uk)

★ **Parkinson's**, a disease of the nervous system, affects 1.5 million Americans. An estimated one in a hundred of all people 60 years and over have Parkinson's. (Check this at www.parkinson.org or www.parkinsons.org.uk)

★ One in every 2000 Caucasian babies has **cystic fibrosis** and these rarely survive to age 30. (See *Dr Koop.com Medical Encyclopedia* at www.umm.edu or www.cysticfibrosis.co.uk)

★ **Bipolar disorder** (otherwise known as manic depression) is a genetic disorder which involves extremes in moods. About one per cent of the population are thought to suffer from it. There is a strong link between bipolarism and suicide. (See www.bipolar.com)

And there's so much more. We humans like to think we're in control of our lives, and maybe most of the time we are. But without warning it can all go wrong. When storm or cancer or virus or earthquake or mental illness strikes, time and again we're pretty defenceless.

So what is it that's wrong with our world? It's not exactly the sort of living space we'd like. And not the kind of universe you'd expect an all-powerful God to create. Does it have to be this way?

Actually, it's worse. Much, much worse.

The real problem is not just the environment around us and the unpleasantness it unleashes from time to time. That's peanuts – at least, it is compared with the animals that live in this world. And I'm not talking here about the struggle to survive, the need to eat or be eaten, the law of the jungle, the survival of the fittest, or any of those realities of nature. I'm talking of the deviant behaviour of one specific creature.

Have you ever thought what a barbaric, brutish, nasty and vicious species the human race is? Honestly, do you know any other creature that treats its own members like this? Some more snapshots…of misery inflicted by humans on humans.

War

★ Eight and a half million soldiers were killed in the First World War; 21 million were wounded.

★ Fourteen and a half million soldiers were killed in the Second World War. The numbers of wounded and missing in action are too numerous to calculate.

Genocide and dictators

★ It's well known that the Nazis methodically slaughtered an estimated six million Jews, many in concentration camps such as Auschwitz. What is less well known is that at least another six million people are estimated to have perished in the same Holocaust – most of them Slavs, Gypsies and homosexuals.

★ Pol Pot and the Khmer Rouge took control of Cambodia in 1975. Within four years an estimated two million people (approximately 20 per cent of the population) had perished from disease, malnutrition and genocide. Literally overnight, entire cities were emptied, property owning was abolished, money became worthless, homes and families were destroyed, thousands were executed. Cambodia became a nation of slaves. Countless more are still being maimed each year by landmines. (Figures supported by Yale University's Cambodian Genocide Program – see www.yale.edu/cgp/)

★ In the former Yugoslavia, 'ethnic cleansing' resulted in over 200,000 people being killed and a further two million being deported or forced to leave their country. Over 700 prison camps and detention facilities were set up, more than 20,000 women systematically raped and 150 mass graves have been uncovered. This so-called ethnic cleansing was carried out with a brutality and savagery designed to instil terror in the civilian population. Some of those evicted from their homes were forced to walk across minefields, others into the face of military offensives.

★ Since 1963, nearly 250,000 people have been killed in

Burundi. In next-door Rwanda, an estimated 500,000 to one million people have been slaughtered since April 1994. The majority of these deaths have been among the Tutsi minority. The mass extermination of Tutsis was carried out primarily by Hutu elements in a concerted, planned, systematic and methodical way. The motivation was tribal hatred. (Source: Neil Weiner, independent researcher and writer, graduate of Princeton's Woodrow Wilson School of Public and International Affairs, in a background briefing paper published on the net (http://www.backgroundbriefing. com/hutututs.html)

Famine and dictators

★ In 1932 a famine began in parts of the USSR that resulted in the deaths of millions of peasants. But it wasn't a famine caused by nature; this one was deliberate and manmade. Josef Stalin was starving the farmers who resisted his collectivisation programme. Troops seized grain and livestock, and prevented trains carrying food from reaching the Ukraine and the Caucasus – the areas where these vast numbers of people were dying. (As well as Compton's see www.infoukes.com)

★ Between 1968 and 1974 some 30 nations sent food to West Africa to aid famine victims. However, most never reached the people who needed it because of the corruption of local officials, poor roads and the lack of advance planning. Half a million people died, as did an estimated 50 million cattle.

★ In 1973, 100,000 Ethiopians died from drought. The plight of these people was hidden from other countries by Emperor Haile Selassie, because he didn't want to endanger the tourist trade to Ethiopia.

Child labour and child prostitution

★ Though it is incredibly difficult to get reliable statistics in this area, an estimated 11 million children (aged four to 14) work, many in brutal and squalid conditions in Pakistani factories, despite laws banning such exploitation. Most are 'purchased' from poor families. As one wealthy landowner has remarked, 'Children are cheaper to run than tractors and smarter than oxen'.

★ Worldwide, an estimated 200 million children under the age of 14 are deprived of freedom, childhood, education and play – forced to work fulltime, frequently in inhumane conditions.

★ Some estimates claim that there are at least one million children in prostitution at this moment in Asia alone.

★ About 300,000 children around the globe served as soldiers in 1999; many were killed in combat or forced to kill others, and committed atrocities on their own or on threat of death. (Human Rights Watch 1999 report)

Landmines (information from the Landmine Data Base, Department of Humanitarian Affairs, United Nations)

★ Described as 'mass death in slow motion', landmines kill or maim over 25,000 civilians every year.

★ 70,000 people in Angola, out of a total population of ten million, are amputees as a result of landmines.

★ It is estimated that there are between 65 million and 200 million uncleared landmines in 62 nations.

Religious persecution (source: *Their Blood Cries Out* by
Paul Marshall (Word) 1997 – Egypt pp15,16; China pp76,77;
Iran pp26–28)

★ Young Egyptian Christian girls are regularly abducted by
militant Muslims, raped and disfigured by having acid
thrown in their faces – until they are prepared to wear the
traditional Islamic veil and convert to Islam. As many as
10,000 Christians have been forced to convert to Islam in
the past few years.

★ China, one of the most repressive states in the world, deals
with its religious and political dissidents through the little-
known and little-publicised *laojiao* (re-education labour
camps). These allow for brutal forms of detention without
trial or hearing. While the Chinese authorities have stated
that about 120,000 prisoners are in *laojiao*, the actual
number is thought to be much higher. They are essentially
concentration camps. Executions are also practised on a
large scale. In some of these executions the prisoners'
organs are harvested for transplants.

★ Iran, like many rigorously Islamic states, practises
religious apartheid. Jews, Bah'ais and Christians are not
only treated with contempt but are also regarded as being
counter-revolutionary – an accusation that leads to the
death penalty. Consequently, non-Muslims have been
brutally repressed since the Iranian revolution of 1979.
Here, too, anyone converting from Islam is subject to the
death penalty.

Slavery

★ In the republic of Mauritania, tens of thousands of blacks
still live as slaves to their Arab-Berber masters, even
though slavery is technically illegal. Slaves are given as
wedding gifts, traded for camels, guns or trucks, and

inherited. The children of slaves belong to the master, and slaves who displease their masters or attempt escape are sometimes tortured and killed in the most brutal manner imaginable. (Check it out in *Disposable People: New Slavery in the Global Economy* by Kevin Bales, the foremost world expert on modern slavery. In this Bales says that 'There are more slaves alive today than all the people stolen from Africa in the time of the transatlantic slave trade'. Fifteen to 20 million are kept in bonded labour in India, Pakistan, Bangladesh and Nepal.)

★ As part of the civil war raging in Sudan, Arab militias armed by the government raid villages in the south, killing the men and taking the women and children. They are kept as personal property, or marched north and sold through auctions, for an average price of $US15. Repeated rape, branding and degradation are par for the course. Some have their Achilles tendons cut so they cannot run away. (See *Their Blood Cries Out* by Paul Marshall, pp17–20,21, and also Human Rights Watch www.hrw.org)

Torture

★ Since 1949 tens of thousands of Tibetans have died after being tortured in Chinese prisons in Tibet. China has effectively outlawed freedom of speech, assembly and religion. Authorities continue to crack down on Tibetans who question Chinese rule, relying on imprisonment and torture in an attempt to eradicate Tibetan religion, culture and nationality. Death by torture and other means has been a fact of life in Tibet since the occupation. The International Campaign for Tibet states that 'Torture often includes beatings, suspension by the arms, electric shock to the mouth and genitals, exposure to intense cold, and rape'. Alexander Solzhenitsyn described China's rule in Tibet as 'more brutal and inhumane than any other communist regime in the world'.

★ Black African slaves in Mauritania are subjected to dreadful torture for even the slightest fault. Apart from the standard beatings, denial of food, prolonged exposure to the sun with hands and feet tied together, castration or branding, many are given ghastly torture such as:

◆ 'The camel treatment' – A person is wrapped around the belly of a dehydrated camel and tied there. The camel is then given water until its belly expands enough to tear the victim apart.

◆ 'The insect treatment' – Insects are put in a slave's ears. The ears are then waxed shut. The arms and the legs are bound. The victim goes insane from the bugs eating into his head.

◆ 'The burning coals'– A slave is laid flat with his legs spread out. He is then buried in sand up to his waist, until he cannot move. Coals are placed between his legs and are burnt slowly. Eventually the legs, thighs and sexual organs of the victim are destroyed.

★ Among the general information in Amnesty International's book *A glimpse of hell: reports on torture worldwide*, edited by Duncan Forrest for Amnesty UK, is 'men and women have truncheons, bottles or electric batons pushed into the anus... pliers are used to pull off finger or toenails, dental drills are used to attack teeth, and acid or caustic substances are poured over the skin. Many corpses are discovered with evidence that before death they suffered horrendous mutilation such as having the ears, hands, genitals or tongue cut off or eyes gouged out.' The book also records mock executions and electric shock treatments, usually concentrated on the genitals, nipples or lips.

Men or monsters?

What sort of monsters do these vile things? I don't know about you but when I read of atrocities like these, I'd like to take the people who do them by the throat and strangle them. Better still, I'd like to put them through the hell they've made for others.

Then I stop and look at myself, and I realise, 'Maybe if I do that, I'm no better than them'. But, at the very least, for all the horror that they've brought to others, they surely deserve to be punished.

And yet… it seems that God doesn't do a thing. He doesn't destroy them. He doesn't punish them. He doesn't even simply halt them in their tracks!

Those statistics, of course, are not isolated examples of human depravity. They are samples only – of an extraordinary range of methods humans have developed through the ages, in order to bring deliberate pain and misery to countless others. If you've done any reading of history, including current history, you'll know that this chapter is striking not so much for the horrors it mentions, as for the long, weary list of brutality that it *fails* to mention.

And the figures just go on accumulating. More and more of them. Human misery flashing across our television sets and scattered through our newspapers and magazines. See enough of it and it becomes a blur. Hear enough of it and it becomes normal. We end up blasé about the huge suffering that engulfs this world. That is, until we become a victim, or one of our loved ones does. That's when the mind-boggling statistics suddenly spring to life. That's when they become much more than just numbers.

Each of the statistics listed above, and thousands more, represents precious human lives – just like you and me. And that's not the end of it. Think how many others are caught up in the suffering or death of each of these victims. Family, close friends, those who viewed it – it soon becomes clear that while each incident of suffering is only a drop in the lake of humanity, it creates ripples that spread throughout the world.

On first impression we might be tempted to believe that things are actually getting better. We are, after all, living in a civilized age. We have democracy and the United Nations and international law...

Sadly, the facts betray this hope. The truth may be that the twentieth century has managed to outdo all the previous nineteen put together. It surely saw more brutality and more raw aggression committed against people than any previous century. Despots such as Hitler, Stalin, Amin, Mao and Pol Pot have had a field day. But while they've been hogging the headlines, petty tyrants like Mussolini and Papa Doc and Ceaucescu and Milosevic and Pinochet have been carrying out murder and rape in their own little corners. Militant fundamentalism across the religions has been on the rise, genocide has found new meaning as a word, racism has plumbed new depths. Religious persecution, despite being rarely reported, is more widespread now than ever before.

And, lest we think that terrorism and brutality are limited to bold headlines and grand butchery, let's not forget that they are also a routine part of life in every nation. Murder, rape and aggravated robbery are common crimes in all countries.

The twentieth century began with the 'war to end all wars'. A few hundred wars later it ended in the mass graves of Kosovo. One hundred years of human violence, atrocity and evil.

Who's to blame?

What are we to make of this? Who's responsible for the mess? You may like to join my friends who blame it on God. After all, they have a pretty good case! Here we have a Being who claims to be the Designer and Creator and Maintainer of this world... and we've just come up with a list – an abbreviated one, at that – of the appalling viciousness that he tolerates.

Why does he allow it? Is this what he calls running the world? Why doesn't he punish the offenders? If this is his idea of good government, it's time he was exposed, accused, impeached, sacked, lynched...

God is in the dock. How does he plead?

3: The tiger inside

 A belief in a supernatural source of evil is not necessary; men alone are quite capable of every wickedness.

Joseph Conrad in *Under Western Eyes*

Yes… well…

I may have ended the last chapter with a rush of blood to the head, and I'm not sure that I want to face the consequences. Put God in the dock? One thing I've learnt – don't take God lightly! So before we go blundering into rash action that we might regret, let's stand back and think this through clearly.

The trouble with putting God in the dock is that he may not stay there! I have this uncomfortable feeling that, instead of defending himself, he might turn the heat on us!

Who do you think you are? You upstart humans accuse me, and all the time it's you who do the murdering and torturing and exploiting. What about your political corruption that creates dictatorships? What about your greed that rapes the planet? What about your insane appetites that make children into prostitutes? You say you feel shocked? Do you know how I feel? I'll tell you what it does to me, this behaviour of yours. It sickens me.

It's true; I'm putting words into God's mouth. But still, before we launch into judicial proceedings maybe we should look at the evidence more carefully. It might just be that we should cast our net a little wider. By looking more closely at *ourselves*.

How much do we humans contribute to this problem of pain? I don't mean just the Hitlers and Pol Pots. Nor am I talking only of murderers and torturers, the greedy and the corrupt. Yes, they're guilty enough. But the more I've puzzled through this problem, the more I've come to realise that you and I are part of what's going on here.

This is going to take some explaining. Bear with me while I try. To get an angle on it, let me begin with one of the particularly ugly things that humans do – the exploitative employment of children. I wrote this next story after browsing the Internet, where I discovered some heartless true-life accounts of how we abuse the future citizens of Planet Earth. I have set this story in a village in Pakistan – but the agony is repeated throughout many countries.

The trap of child labour

Picture the scene. It's a sweltering morning in the small Punjabi village. A carpet master, Saleem, is talking over with a young man named Mukhtar the advantages his son will enjoy as an apprentice weaver.

* * *

'Your son Suleman is bright and could go far,' Saleem says. 'I've had my eye on him for several months. Just half a year at the loom in my factory and he'll learn far more than he would do in six years of school. As you know, I only employ the best, the most experienced craftsmen. Your boy will be in good hands, taught all the traditional skills. As he improves, well, his pay will rise. Take my word for it, Suleman will thank you for giving him this excellent opportunity. Your whole family will bless you for your wisdom.'

Saleem's words are well rehearsed. He's constantly recruiting for his workshops. It pays him to seek out boys aged seven to 10. He admits himself that they are ideal employees. Their fingers are dextrous; they have the stamina to work long hours; they are obedient, even eager to please. Many of them are quite willing to work round the clock for him when he's under pressure to get out a particular consignment of carpets. Even better, they are economical to employ. For what he pays one second-class adult weaver he can get three boys, sometimes four, turning out first-class work in no time.

Overall, the low cost of child labour gives Saleem and his fellow manufacturers a significant advantage in the Western marketplace, where they undercut their competitors from countries prohibiting child labour, often by improbable amounts. And it's hardly surprising that American and European consumers are attracted to low price, high quality products, so that imports of child-made carpets from Pakistan have trebled in the past two decades. To satisfy increasing demand, Pakistan's carpet makers have expanded production at existing factories and opened new ones as fast as they can. It makes economic sense to have as many children in the workforce as possible; some factories are entirely run using child workers. Somewhere between 500,000 and one million Pakistani children aged four to 14 work as full-time carpet weavers. UNICEF believes that they make up 90 per cent of the carpet makers' workforce.

Saleem is persuasive, delivering his speech at volume and with a theatrical display of hand gestures, shrugs and raised eyebrows. He smiles broadly. Just in case Mukhtar does not fully appreciate his generosity, he adds, 'If only my father had given me such an opportunity... '

Mukhtar hesitates. No doubt this is partly because his son Suleman is just seven years old. Some of his neighbour's children have been working in similar carpet workshops and he is not sure they are really that happy, not really earning that much money...

He nervously return's Saleem's smile. 'Of course, every father wants the best for such a fine son. He is indeed a good worker, he will learn quickly... perhaps one day he will be a journeyman weaver... maybe even have a workshop of his own...' His voice fades.

In truth, whatever misgivings Mukhtar has are overshadowed by his crippling poverty. He has to keep a family of five by working at a nearby kiln, moulding bricks by hand for up to 80 hours a week. At the best of times the pay is poor; sometimes there is no pay at all. For example, just a couple of weeks earlier the monsoon rains destroyed several thousand unfired bricks that had been left out to dry in the factory grounds. The kiln owner insisted that the workers take responsibility for the damage and refused to pay them for the time it took to make replacements for the lost bricks - two whole weeks.

Mukhtar is now several months behind with the rent, and in debt to the village moneylender. Talking it over with his wife, bonding their eldest son to Saleem seemed the only possible way out of their spiralling debt. Saleem, pointed out Mukhtar's wife, was prosperous and his workshop was not too far from their village. At the well that day the women had been saying how desperately short he was of child workers. Surely that would mean he would be willing to pay a good price?

True, Saleem's workshop is always in need of more children. But Saleem is unwilling to pay more than he has to; in fact he doesn't see why he should even pay the market rates.

'Business is not so good at the moment. Five thousand rupees for five years. That's a fair offer. If business improves later this year, well, perhaps there'll be another couple of hundred. Many fathers would be glad to get half this amount for an inexperienced boy.'

Mukhtar swallows, trying to hide his distress. He's being offered a paltry sum - about two months' earnings for an adult weaver. He was hoping for something three or four times higher. He rubs his hands together, anxiously. He is a slight figure, stooped and worn thin from his years at the kiln even though still a young man. His skin is pemanently marked with soot, his ragged tunic blackened. Though something inside him wants to protest, he remains acutely aware of his caste, and that dictates that he speak with reverence to Saleem. In the most self-deprecating terms he knows he suggests that his son's pay might be increased by another thousand rupees.

'Sir, my family will always be indebted to you. We will remember you constantly in our prayers as our benefactor, the one who rescues us.'

Flattered, Saleem agrees, proferring a manicured hand. He can afford this little generosity. The money he pays to Mukhtar will be paid in small instalments, from which he will deduct a range of inflated and contrived costs for the boy's training and maintenance, his food, his tools, any materials he spoils by mistake. Mukhtar will discover that he is fortunate if he actually receives one third of the promised sum. But for now he is ignorant of these deductions and unwilling to ask questions which might complicate things. The deal is sealed with a shake of the hands and a first instalment of 200 rupees. There is no contract. No witness.

Saleem confirms the stark reality of the agreement.

'Your boy belongs to me now. Make sure he understands that he is answerable only to me from now on. My needs and the needs of my business have absolute priority over those of his family. He must know that he must commit himself to pleasing me in all he does.'

Mukhtar bows low, repeats his gratitude, and runs off to find Suleman.

So reasonable

It all sounds so reasonable…

What upsets me most about Saleem is that he makes it all sound so reasonable. And I have a nasty feeling that *that* is part of the whole problem. Doesn't every one of us come up with convincing explanations for the things we do, especially some of our behaviour that might be just a little bit grubby if only we allowed ourselves to look at it?

I mean, we can all see that Saleem is a slimeball underneath. My problem is that I wonder if we aren't all slimeballs! Yes, sure, you and I don't do anything as sleazy as Saleem's little scheme. But, in our own way, don't we have plenty of skeletons in our cupboards?

Before we start pointing the finger at the tyrants and the racists and the terrorists and the exploiters of this world, maybe we should stop and think about the pain and suffering in our own living rooms. The truth is, evil is not just done out there, but inside *us*. In *our* hearts and lives. Every day, each of us causes pain to someone else. We do it in a thousand different ways. A putdown, a thoughtless uncaring action, an unnecessarily harsh or cruel comment, a selfish decision or revengeful act, a gossipy quip or ungracious slur.

Each of these self-centred acts may sound of little account in itself. But they cause greater or lesser hurt to somebody. And when you put them together – hundreds of such actions by each of us over the weeks and months – think of the immeasurable pain we cause one another.

Right here is where this whole accusation against God turns nasty. Because you and I are in the firing line. In a thousand ways, little and large, we have caused hurt and unhappiness to the people around us. I don't know about you, but I'm ready to admit that sometimes (okay... frequently) I've deliberately hurt others – with words or looks or actions. When I face up to this, what makes me feel sick is that often the ones I've treated shabbily are those I love most. I dread to think what damage my own children will carry with them into adulthood – grievances that I've caused, sometimes knowingly, sometimes in ignorance. I can't tell you what all of my failings are, but I'm sure that my wife and children could put together quite a list.

Consider this: family breakups are at a crisis level in our society; divorce rates are at an all-time high, the fallout from such separations is all around us. As symptoms of our destructive homes, youth suicide rates are way above other age groups, and children are committing more and more petty crimes... even violent ones.

So let's begin here. A while back we asked the question... why doesn't God punish the offenders?

Is part of the answer that... you and I are offenders?

Let's be personal. What do you want God to do about *my* failures?

(It's some small comfort to me – though not much – to know that for each accusation you make against me, you may find yourself admitting to a similar charge!)

Perhaps I can best explain what I mean by telling a story. It starts at home, and it's about an experience that is becoming more and more frequent these days. In telling this story, I've tried to get behind the events and into the feelings. Tell me, have I managed to get close to the truth?

* * *

When parents separate

The sunset looked spectacular against the snow-covered mountain backdrop. But Justin didn't even notice. Instead he was churning over the conversation with Sarah that afternoon. Most of all, her parting shot: 'You're an insecure little rat!'

She had no right to say that. Justin had exploded with anger at her words and stormed out. He winced again as he thought about it – how she'd put her finger right on a sore spot, even though she knew nothing of his pain. He wasn't about to make himself vulnerable, with her or anyone. The last time he did that he got horribly hurt.

Like a child prodding at a loose tooth, Justin pushed his mind back into the anguish of earlier years and memories. Things had been good for the first seven years of his life. Growing up in the suburbs of Auckland was a lot of fun. Always other kids to play with, places to explore. What he remembered most fondly were the summer holidays at the beach up north. Going out on the boat with Dad, cricket on the beach with the cousins, Dad cooking the barbecue with the whole extended family around. Mum laughing and joking. Water fights.

Precious memories. But soon after Justin began his third year at school, everything began to go wrong. Actually things had started to sour between his parents long before then, but being only seven Justin had not really noticed. First there were the arguments – mostly at night after he'd gone to bed. Then the icy silences at mealtimes.

And he could remember when Dad started coming home late at night. Since he left early each morning for work, that meant that Justin often went days on end without even seeing him.

Justin prodded further into the pain. He loved his father. Dad was the best. So not being able to do things with him was lousy. And even when he was around, he seemed so wrapped up in himself. For some reason that Justin couldn't understand, times with Dad began to be disappointing.

His parents' arguments grew worse. Then the noise of slammed doors and glass hurled against walls. One night Justin heard the car start up after an argument. He remembered going to sleep with the sound of his mother's heart-sobs through the wall. Dad didn't come home for a week that time. It felt like an eternity. It was an eternity for a boy of seven.

And then the fateful day. Justin and his sisters were brought into the room together. They were told that their parents couldn't live together any more. Dad would be moving out. Like a photo frame frozen in time, Justin pictured again his own shock and disbelief. He remembered how his older sister Mary ran to her room, slamming the door, crying uncontrollably, shouting 'No! No! No!' Justin sat motionless, not saying a word. At that moment his whole world fell apart. Shattered into small pieces.

Mum and Dad... they both tried to comfort him and his sisters... told them how they still loved them... always would, and that life would be okay. But the words had a hollow ring and Justin knew inside that they weren't true. Outwardly he showed no emotion, said nothing. Inwardly he was a world of confusion, anger, hurt and fear.

He recalled the fortnightly visits with his Dad. How the car would pull up. How he'd jump in with eager anticipation. The messing about in his father's flat. And then the agony of going home on Sunday afternoons. The numbness of being torn apart. Feeling guilty about wanting to stay. Not that he didn't love Mum. It was the pain of being tugged in two directions.

Justin shook himself. Why was he thinking back over all this? Recalling the hurts never helped. He was 16 now and life had moved on. 'Can't dwell on the past,' he reminded himself.

Truth was that deep down the pain was too intense to be disturbed. Like a festering boil, even a small touch could set off fire in his body. Better to let it alone. Forget about it. Move on. Problem was... the pain wouldn't go away.

Justin glanced out the window again and noticed a young boy skimming stones on the lake with his father. A thousand images came to mind. Like a dentist's drill they touched a raw nerve. He began to cry – great, gulping sobs flowed from a heart broken by the loss of experiences he'd had ever-so-briefly with his Dad, and then lost. Each cry brought to the surface more pain, more grief.

'Why d'you have to go, Dad? Why? Why couldn't we all live together? For always... '

* * *

Who are the victims?

It's sad enough, what Justin has gone through. But the sadness is magnified when you realise how many children – in your own suburb alone – are torn apart just like that. What right do their parents have to dump that misery on them? On children who can't do anything about it? On children who can't understand it.

On children who are scared spectators of a split they blame themselves for…

Who's really to blame for the knife that twists in Justin's heart? Who should be punished?

Blame? Punishment? But hang on. Justin's parents are victims too. So why are we talking punishment? Haven't those two suffered enough? Why do we want to add more to the weight of their misery? Don't they, too, deserve our sympathy?

They surely do. They are victims of a broken relationship. A wrecked marriage is a heartbreak that I wouldn't wish on anyone.

And yet, is it that simple? Are we to ignore what was done to Justin and his sisters? Don't they have a legitimate grievance against their parents? Weren't those children dropped, through no fault of their own, into a cruel situation? In fact, couldn't we go further? Time and time again, the teenagers and young adults who cause crime and destruction are products of broken homes. When innocent citizens become victims, when police and social workers get dragged in – all of them are caught up in damage that was done long before. They carry the can for parents who failed their children. Doesn't *society* have a grievance against those parents?

The last thing I want to do is condemn parents. But there's an ugly truth here. As much as each of us is a victim of pain, large or small… we also *cause* pain. *We* hurt, and then we pass the hurt on to others.

It's not easy for any of us to acknowledge, but if we are serious about finding answers to the age-old question of suffering and evil, this surely must be included in the equation: that you and I have caused some of it. I'm not saying we're in the same league as the Hitlers and Milosevics of this world. Just accepting that not all the blame is 'out there'.

Until we've faced up to that, we're not ready to ask the question, 'Why doesn't God do something about it?'

4: Designer world

 Everyone wants to change the world, but no one wants to change themselves.

Tolstoy

Thanks for sticking with me. The last chapter wasn't easy for me to write, and I'm not exactly sure where it leaves us. But I do know that we can't grapple with our accusations against God until we've at least identified our own guilt.

Okay, we've done that. Now, I think, we're ready to raise the big question. *Why doesn't God do something about it?*

We've toyed with putting God himself in the dock. On the face of it, that's an appealing line of attack. But, knowing what we now know, perhaps we should look more closely at what we're asking him to do.

Are we wanting God to be Policeman Of The World? If we are... okay, then I suppose it makes some sort of sense that he should instantly correct any injustice that occurs. But if we're seriously to take that approach, then we'd better face up to some practical problems it produces...

For example, at what point should God intervene? When a thug rapes a 14-year-old girl? Yes, I guess most of us would go along with that. When the class bully snatches lunch off another student and punches his face until it bleeds? Uh-huh. When a street kid steals a loaf of bread? When a neighbour insults you? When your sister slams the door in your face? When your father annoys you by telling the same story over again? When *you* lose your temper with a member of your family?

Time for you to put your theories on the line. (After all, you chose to read this book!) What 'crime' is sufficiently bad to involve God? And when he does get involved, how should he deal with the offender? I mean, would you like to have the rapist exterminated? That would certainly stop him from destroying the lives of other young women. Are we talking here about an electric shock for the bully, maybe? And what would be an appropriate response to *your* temper tantrum...?

I'm inviting you to design a world. To be fair, that's a big job and takes a long time, so we'll dispense with the geography and physics and things. For today, let's just concentrate on law and order.

This marvellous world that you would like to see – how do you want to organise it? In particular, how will you make sure that the inhabitants of your universe treat one another with the respect and courtesy that you want?

Let me introduce you to the *Creation Control Computer*. It's a sophisticated device, incredibly fast, and unbelievably powerful. It will instantly process your ideas. All you have to do is decide what level of behaviour control you want to impose on the creatures of your world; then choose your settings. Once you've made your decisions, it only remains to press the Enter key, and the Universe-As-You'd-Like-It-To-Be will begin.

Ready?

Designer world

Designer's Name: ....
(Please enter your name here so we know who to blame.)

Social control

How will you ensure the good behaviour of your created beings?

> Will you design them so that individuals can never cause pain or hurt to others? ☐

> Or will you give to each person control of his/her own behaviour? ☐

Don't rush lightly past this decision. It's the key to all that will follow. If you choose option 1, you realise what you're making, don't you? I don't want to butt in on your creation buzz but, to put it crudely... do you want people, or toys? You may be satisfied with talking dolls which walk when you say walk and talk when you say talk. Or you might be looking for something more... well, interesting. (I just raise this point because you're going to be stuck with these creatures for a few aeons. Or at least until you get sick of them and toss them into your cosmic bottom drawer. Up to you, of course.)

Policing your planet

How will you ensure that your created beings observe your rules of behaviour?

> Will you monitor each individual yourself? ☐

Or will you give to them the responsibility for controlling unsocial behaviour among themselves? □

Or will you operate a self-correcting system, where a creature that offends automatically stops functioning? □

Or do you have some other brilliant idea? □

Punishment

How will your creatures be disciplined? What form of punishment will you use?

Physical pain responses? □

Awareness of their mistakes and mental anguish about their negative behaviour? □

Other? □

Culpability

How much wrong must someone do before receiving punishment?

Will punishment be allotted at the first offence? □

Or after two or three offences? □

Or not till your created being becomes a habitual offender? □

Case study: David is a teacher who becomes cynical about the youngsters he teaches. Among other things, he resorts to sarcasm as a way of cutting kids down to size. Should David be punished the first time he does this? Or when he has repeated the sarcasm three or four times? Or not till it has established itself as a regular part of his personality?

Mitigating circumstances

What allowance will you make for past suffering that has produced a person's present behaviour?

Case study: Carl was bullied and physically abused as a child. How do you intend dealing with him when he loses control and thrashes his own two-year-old?

No excuses? ☐

Percentage reduction in punishment levels? (In which case, will you allow the same leniency when Carl's son beats up *his* son? And then when *he* beats up *his* son. And then when...) ☐

An adjustment period during which Carl must bring his behaviour up to scratch. (And what about the damage done to Carl's son in the meantime?) ☐

Time frame

When your creatures commit a wrong, when will they suffer the consequences of their behaviour?

Immediately, right when they're offending? ☐

At the end of each day... or month... or year? ☐

At the end of their life? ☐

In an afterlife? ☐

Case study: While coaching his football team of 10-year-olds, Brian loses his temper and swears at Johnny. Will you give him an immediate jab of pain in his gut? Or will you allow him time to mull over his actions and to realise himself what he has done? You might want to allow him the opportunity to apologise to Johnny, for example. If he does, will you reduce the punishment, or perhaps revoke it altogether? (Mind you, how genuine will apologies be if everyone knows they'll be zapped if they don't make them?) And if he does apologise, what plans do you have for healing the damage he's done to Johnny?

Forgiveness

A tricky one, this. Will you allow punishment to be revoked if a person comes to admit to past wrong behaviour?

Case study: Anne was so aggressive in pursuing money, advancement, personal fame and a flashy home that she treated her two daughters as annoying intrusions into her life. When they were on the verge of adolescence, she suddenly saw what she was doing, and what her children had missed out on. With a vigour equal to her previous failings, she set about giving love and attention to the two unparented girls.

Will you wipe the slate clean and allow her to start afresh?

Will you still punish her for the harm she has done?

How will you deal with the girls and the damage they suffered as a result of the years of lost parenting?

Related decision: Will you allow Hitler (who, you'll remember, engineered the deaths of more than 14 million combatants and an incalculable number of noncombatants) the chance to experience forgiveness?

Perhaps you'd prefer a system of punishments and perks. If so, how will you handle this balance between punishing and forgiving?

By a smack for every bad deed and a kiss for every good one? ☐

By calculations on a scale of good and bad behaviour? ☐

Related decision: Does one good act cancel out one bad one? If Sally ends the day with a score of 85 credits and 79 demerits, does she qualify for an award... or a beating?

That's all. Simple, wasn't it? Now it just remains for you to tap the Enter key and a whole universe of suffering – or non-suffering, depending on your creative skills, though I'm not going to hold my breath – will grind into action.
   Oops, sorry, one last thing...
   Please enter here options available to your creatures for filing complaints:

Swear, rant and rave. ☐

Revoke sacrifices made to you. ☐

Destroy your world in a nuclear holocaust. ☐

Freedom to choose

Seriously... do we really want to be zapped every time we offend? Just imagine what it would be like if God did set up a world where he intervened each time someone stepped out of line. It could be distinctly uncomfortable – not just for the thugs, but also for ordinary, 'decent' people. I suspect that under a God-driven, cause-and-effect world, we would find ourselves dealt with on a very regular basis!

The truth is that if God did use that sort of approach, our free will would be destroyed. It would take only a few zaps and we would quickly become as conditioned as Pavlov's dogs. Our apologies would be empty ones, our contrition would be meaningless, our behaviour would be slavish. Isn't it fortunate for us that, in his wisdom, God has chosen a more 'hands-off' approach than the quick-fix one that we so often demand!

Tell me something. As you mulled over which settings you would choose for your world, did it occur to you that the whole approach was flawed? That if you made a race of thinking creatures, the very idea of constantly punishing them was somehow self-defeating? If your universe is to give you any satisfaction at all, don't you really want it to be a society of beings who are intelligent and responsible?

Could this explain why God has chosen not to put his creatures under instant control? Could it be that the very idea is at odds with his whole concept of a human race?

One thing is for sure. From what we see around us, clearly God did not opt for a world of robots. One of the things that make us human is our ability to choose how we will respond to any given situation. In the world you and I occupy, this is a God-given freedom. With all sorts of consequences that run deeply through our lives.

Let me choose an example. Though God is a mystery to us, one striking thing we do know about him is that he has created us with the capacity to love. Yet... *love cannot exist where it is enforced by punishments.*

I suggest that when God chose to make us capable of loving

each other – and of loving him – his hand was forced. He had no choice. He had to give us total freedom, including the freedom to hate. Anything else would be a cheap imitation of love. And if that is true of love, it is also true of justice... kindness... loyalty... courage... honour... generosity... compassion...

Well, you see what I'm saying. Take away human freedom and you take from our world all that makes it human. All that makes it worthwhile. Why bother playing creators if you're just making toys?

Another way?

Yes, but is there another way?

Okay, freedom seems to be basic to our human life. But does that mean we have to have pain and suffering as well? Surely they are not necessary parts of living? Surely we could have a world without them?

We've reached a crucial question. What's the point of pain? Why do we need it? Couldn't there be some other way of regulating this world? Why open the door to such colossal misery?

It's not only a crucial question, it's also a tantalising one. Does anyone understand pain? How do you make sense of it? I've gone hunting for an answer, and what I've found has taken me by surprise...

5: When no pain is a prison

 Those things that hurt, instruct.

Benjamin Franklin

The time has come to look more deeply at the problem of suffering. Before we go any further we need to ask this question: What would it be like if we *did* live in a world without pain?

If my children were to grow up without experiencing the hurts and mishaps of life, what sort of people would they become? I have this uneasy feeling that they might be pretty shallow adults. Think of the human failures we sometimes read about. You know the sort: children of royal families who were given their own way all the time, then, when they finally inherited the kingdom or empire or whatever it was they were born to, they turned out to be disasters. If you want a few names from history, it isn't hard to find them – monsters like Caligula, the Roman Emperor whose three short years of rule were marked by savage brutality. Or misfits like Marie Antoinette, who had no idea about real life. (She's the one who, when she heard that starving peasants had no bread to eat, said 'Let them eat cake'.)

And you don't have to go back in history. Think of the children of modern-day millionaires who have everything given to them. They're a byword for adults who end up as spendthrifts and hopeless failures.

Where does all this fit in to our human dilemma? Does it have any relevance to the universal problem of suffering and pain? What got me thinking along these lines was one of those quiet heroes of the twentieth century – a man by the name of Paul Brand.

* * *

'Thank God for pain'

Dr Paul Brand, a skilled surgeon, has done what most of us would love to do. He has personally changed for the better the lives of many thousands of people. Operations and therapies which he developed are now standard throughout the world.

So when he says, 'Thank God for pain... ' it may sound crazy, but he's worth listening to. You see, he's spent his life working with people who can't feel pain! People who suffer from leprosy.

The germs of leprosy attack the nerves that transmit pain. Therefore a person with leprosy can have what ought to be a painful experience – a burn, or a cut, or a thorn in the hand, or a speck of dirt in the eye – and never know.

'For a normal person,' says Dr Brand, 'pain takes priority. It dominates your life until you deal with it. If you get a piece of grit in your eye you'll abandon whatever you're doing – an interesting conversation or an urgent piece of work – until you get rid of it.

'That's why you and I have two eyes today. My patients, who have lost the feeling of pain, do nothing about that piece of grit, unless it gets in the way of their vision. Then they may rub their eye, perhaps – and scratch it without knowing that they're harming themselves. The result is that they go blind.

'If they get a thorn in their foot (in countries like India, many of them walk around barefoot) they just go on walking. They don't even limp. And the thorn gets driven deeper. Then the foot becomes infected, they get an abscess, the foot swells and becomes red... but they go on walking without a limp. They don't spare it at all.

'That drives the pus into the bones and into the tendon sheaths. It spreads all up and down until finally the foot is destroyed – not by leprosy but simply by the effect of the thorn.'

People who suffer from leprosy have to learn to avoid danger. Paul Brand tells a story about a special patient he had trained...

'He was so good at avoiding injury that in the Detection Centre he would go a month at a time without damaging his hands or his feet. And he taught others to do it – just by constant forethought and alertness. He had originally been thrown out of his home when he caught leprosy. But now he was cured he decided to go back for a weekend to see how he could handle it on the outside.

'The first night he lay down on his mattress on the floor and was just delighted to be able to sleep in his own home.

'But in the morning when he woke up... the back of his index finger was missing. It had been chewed off in the night by a rat.

'He just wept. He was so angry at himself for forgetting that people who can't feel pain must have a cat in the room. We used to breed cats for this purpose and gave them away to our patients for their protection. He'd forgotten to take one home with him.

'So he decided he would stay awake all the next night and hopefully catch the rat or at least avoid being damaged by it. He tried to keep from sleeping by reading a book with a hurricane lantern beside him. He managed to stay awake till about four o'clock in the morning. But then he was just too sleepy and his eyes shut. The book dropped and his hand fell to the side... and rested against the hot glass of the hurricane lantern until morning!

'When he came back to me on Monday he had one finger partially eaten by a rat and the skin on the back of the other hand destroyed by a burn. We were able to repair those things. We gave him a skin graft and he's fine now. But he was in terrible distress. He told me, "I feel I'm in prison. A prison of no pain. I just dare not do half the things you do."

'I'll never forget his words: "It's pain that frees you."

'That's why I believe pain is a gift from God.'

★ ★ ★

A powerful insight

When you get insights like that (taken from *Grapevine* magazine, a New Zealand publication) – from a victim who has lived with suffering for years, and from a doctor who has spent a life working with people in pain – you'd be foolish to ignore them. They make a powerful point. Pain is a crucial part of our humanity and of our ability to survive. It's not an unfortunate accident in the way we are made.

So let's not superficially abuse God for our pain response. It's a brilliant solution to at least some of our needs – and a powerful piece of evidence exists to show why. Dr Brand was actually commissioned to produce a pain-substitute warning system for people who have no pain response. He successfully did so, using a buzzer that activated when too much pressure was being placed on muscle or nerve. The system worked well… but it proved a failure. Incredibly, the people who used it ignored the warnings!

So we need pain. But of course this doesn't solve for us the problem of 'senseless pain'. Toothache is fine – it warns us to take action against a decaying molar. But multiple sclerosis is a different matter. It brings pain that is a malfunction in our bodies. Same with arthritis – a disease that brings years of purposeless suffering.

So… back again to the vast mystery of suffering! But as we return to it, let's make sure we do understand the part of the picture which Dr Brand has identified. Pain is no mistake. It is an essential part of living on this planet of ours. Without it, we'd be in serious trouble.

6: When God hit back...

If I've understood it right, the choices that we make leave God with a real problem. Every time he sees one of us causing someone else to suffer, he faces an agonising dilemma.

Of course, he could smack us back into line. Only, as we know, he can't. Not when he has deliberately chosen to set up a world where we are genuinely free to make our own choices.

So what's happening? The only explanation I know that covers all the facts is this: God has deliberately chosen to limit his own power. Does that sound absurd? The Almighty God voluntarily deciding to be the Powerless God? It's not as odd as you might think. All around us are human versions of exactly the same choice. Wherever you go you will find caring parents who allow their children to make decisions for themselves – even though both father and mother realise that wrong choices will inevitably be made from time to time.

Why? Because good parents know that their children will never reach a full, healthy and independent maturity unless they learn to take responsibility for their own lives. That's the only proven way of progressing from childhood through adolescence to mature adulthood.

And God knows that that's the only way he can bring us to be the fully human creatures he has designed us to be.

What if he didn't give us that freedom? What if he intervened to stop atrocities and abuse? Would it work?

You and I would argue, no doubt, (after our experimental 'creation' in Chapter 4) that that is the wrong approach altogether. And it so happens we can be even more definite. For, you see, that very scenario has actually occurred. There was a time when God did choose to use his power to halt the growing tide of cruelty and suffering. Once in human history God intervened by displaying his anger at the evil in this world. His raw act of power destroyed all life on this planet, except for a handful of humans and animals riding the raging waters in a boat.

If you're seriously entertaining the idea that God is to blame for the pain and suffering in this world, then think carefully about the effects of the Great Flood. I'm sure you know the story – who hasn't heard of Noah and the Ark? And yet, what was really going on in God's mind?

I've often thought about it. And I've tried to see it from his point of view. Just imagine it...

* * *

The ultimate solution

God's anger had been building for some time. Across the earth his prized creation, humans, had been steadily multiplying, not only in numbers, but in open rebellion. It was an ugly sight, to see thousands of humans thinking they could give God the fingers. Ugly... and pathetic. God's skin was thick enough to cope with that, but there was another problem. The exciting plans he had made for his beloved Earth, the vision he had for life in Paradise – all were in tatters around him.

It had not always been this way. God remembered with sadness the early days, the time when his universe was at peace. What a delight those years had been. And what a creative idea, to shape two beings and to extend to them the relationship of the three-in-one God – Father, Son and Spirit!

Right from the beginning, he had enjoyed the widening of their divine love – sharing it with the Man and the Woman. Evening after evening they would walk together in the Garden and recall the day's experiences. A delightful joy filled their talk as they discussed the ideas Adam and Eve had for managing the Garden.

They were the apple of their Father's eye, those two. It wasn't just that they were happy to cooperate with his plans for them. It was more than that. They loved the whole world he'd created, and they threw themselves enthusiastically into looking after it. They were totally fulfilled.

And, best of all, they loved him in return, loved him simply and honestly. Yes, the Father, Son and Spirit agreed, this sense of contentment from seeing their creation respond was unparalleled by any of their other great projects.

But that was now long past – ever since that fateful day when the Man and the Woman had chosen to go their own way. The Father felt waves of tears well up in his eyes as he remembered the events. In a mood of selfish greed they had suddenly decided to snatch at equality with him, to disobey the one restriction that protected their Paradise. By that step they shattered not just the bond of God's three-in-one love but also the unity of the whole universe. After that act of betrayal, things could never be the same.

God had always known the risk. But he'd accepted it as the price of giving such boundless potential to the Man and Woman. Even now he didn't doubt that it had been worth it. Which only added to the pain of the broken relationship. Each day was a constant reminder of what had been, for a time.

And what might have been, for an eternity.

With the original plan in tatters, Father, Son and Spirit had fallen back on a second initiative. It took into account the new imperfections in the beings they'd created, but even so it offered the prospect of maintaining the link with them. By placing certain boundaries around the Man and the Woman and their offspring, God hoped to protect them from themselves – to save them from their own worst tendencies. While their world would necessarily become more limited, nevertheless it was still God's intention that they be free to love their Creator by choice – even though, of course, that meant they must also be free to spurn him.

So it was a new beginning... of sorts. Sadly, despite God's best preparations, the humans had made a disappointing response. They were clearly feeling crushed and disoriented by the results of their folly. Their very first child eventually succumbed to jealousy and committed murder. Murder of his own brother! Then as time moved on and the human family grew, many of the Man and Woman's descendants stoutly refused to give God the time of day. In fact, they not only treated him with disdain, they soon learned how to create havoc and mistrust among themselves. The growing human race quickly became a cesspool of all that God despised – deceit, greed, dishonesty, pride, apathy, bitterness and murder. As humans fell out with one another and ignored God, their management of the created world grew more and more destructive. Injuries and injustice were universal. Humanity became a festering sore that began to disturb the equilibrium of the whole universe.

And yet, here and there, a few humans stuck with their determination to follow God. The Father couldn't bring himself to abandon them. Enoch was one – and what a delight he was. A human who returned the Father's love so honestly that it was almost like the early days. Here was a model of what could be, despite the rebellion. But Enoch was an exception. There were few who tried seriously to follow in his footsteps.

And now – how much longer should this be allowed to go on? Human behaviour had become so repulsive that the Father couldn't ignore it any more. The outright rebellion seemed to know no limits. Plan A had long ago been destroyed... and Plan B was now in disarray. Few of his creatures gave so much as a second thought to God. While in one sense the shaking of fists by such petty beings was comical, the Father knew he must act. His pain ran deep. He had had such plans for them and yet they were being so stubborn and stupid. Couldn't they see that they were destroying themselves and their world? Couldn't they understand that the Father's standards were there for their own growth and fulfilment?

Of course, there was the other plan, his Son's idea. But God's father heart froze at the very thought of it. No, he could never ask that of his Son. That was too terrible. Things must never be allowed to reach such a desperate situation. He would destroy the humans and scrap the whole idea before that.

So that was it. There was no other reasonable choice. The great adventure of love would have to be abandoned.

And yet... could he be untrue to himself in that way? How could he destroy any human – even if it was only one – who honestly tried? And there was one. A man called Noah. One human who had caught the Father's vision of what life could be. He wasn't perfect, he made mistakes. But his heart was deeply committed to life lived God's way. Like Enoch he brought a deep joy to the Father's heart. Their conversations were often full of warmth and happiness, and reminded God of the way it used to be with the original Man and Woman.

No, he couldn't destroy Noah, nor the family that meant so much to him. Nor anyone else who was willing to stand alongside him. But that decision only made all the more stark the behaviour of the rest. Why should they be allowed to cause such suffering and pain and misery? The atrocities were so shocking that the only way left was to wipe them out.

Noah was typically obedient when the Father instructed him to build a boat. It would take some time and it might look rather strange in his backyard, but God emphasised the importance of the task.

As the months progressed and the strange scheme began to take shape, Noah's neighbours took to taunting him. They hooted when he told them it was a boat – in the middle of a dry plain! They jeered when he explained the Father's plan. Noah secretly admitted to his wife that the absurdity struck him too, but he had long since learned that the Father's ways always made sense.

When the huge boat was finished, God instructed Noah and his family to select animals. Housing them on board was a massive operation. It wasn't exactly the Queen Mary, but Noah had confidence that God knew what he was doing. On the day they elected to close the door, a crowd of locals gathered to ridicule their misguided neighbour. Noah invited aboard anyone who wished to join them. The offer was greeted with a chorus of catcalls. Who did he think he was? Thanks – but no thanks!

With a regretful wave, Noah closed the door, and the crowd dispersed. The rain started that night. Most of the locals didn't think anything of it. After all, it was the wet season. But after three days of constant downpour, flash flooding began to occur. Soon all were fleeing for higher ground, except that in this part of the Middle East high ground was a commodity in short supply.

Through the long interminable days, Noah and his family regularly looked out through the shutters in the side of the boat. In the midst of the devastation they saw one couple hanging on to the roof of a house, wildly shaking their fists at the sky and yelling abuse. Then, as quickly as the blink of an eyelid, they were gone. Utter defiance, right to the end.

Meanwhile, the Father, the Son and the Spirit were shattered. Such drastic measures were the last thing they had ever intended, and the pain was unimaginable. Not just destroying the work of their own hands, but watching such death and despair. The ache in the heart of God went on and on, going deeper and deeper. After what – even to God – seemed an eternity, he called a halt to the storms.

At last the water began to recede. Weeks later the boat eventually came to rest. On the side of a mountain, Noah and his family stumbled out and looked around. Silence. Not a living thing stirred. All was mud-covered desolation. They huddled together and contemplated their future – the future of humanity.

The floodwaters were rapidly receding. Soon valleys that had been under water for months began to sprout new life – grass and trees to re-clothe the mud-stained earth. Then one day, looking skyward, Noah was astonished to see a beautiful, multi-coloured prism of light, stretching right across the horizon. Inwardly he sensed the significance. Never again would the Father use his power to achieve what his love could not. God was announcing that such complete intervention was not the way. The ultimate solution lay in other directions.

✶ ✶ ✶

God's patience

Back in Chapter 4 we played a game about world creating. But this world you and I are in is no game. It's a serious place where sometimes one false step can mean death. Literally. And where one human can do monstrous things to another. It's a chilling thought that right now – at this very moment, as you read this sentence – some sickening brutality is being done to a citizen of this planet. And God has to come to terms with the brutality he has allowed to be visited on one of his creatures. How does he cope with it?

Apparently not by lashing out and blasting the abuser with a thunderbolt. Nor by whipping you and me when we pass on some nasty piece of gossip, or when we mindlessly destroy the bright and innocent curiosity in a child simply because that child annoys us at an inconvenient moment.

Nor by giving up on us and trashing the whole universe.

It seems to me that God's reluctance to act in the same way as he did in the days of Noah isn't because of apathy. It's not that he can't be bothered. Neither does it mean that he's at his wit's end. That he's run out of ideas. Or that he doesn't have the power to act. On the contrary, though there's evidence that God does intervene in human affairs and still uses his power from time to time, fortunately for us it's never in the total way he resorted to back then.

You don't need to be an expert in history to know that God has instead chosen a much gentler – and slower – approach. He has sought to respond to the pain and suffering of this world by offering his love instead. Personally I'm grateful for this sympathetic gentleness. I think it may have spared me a lot of sharp discipline. And also allowed me to grow at a pace I can cope with.

That's the good side. But the downside is that I have to accept a much greater time frame for God's plans. When it comes to helping us mature to the target he has for us, God seems ready to give it plenty of room.

For some people, a lifetime. For some changes, an age.

7: So what's God up to?

I'm beginning to think that if our best response to this problem of suffering is to blame God, then we risk missing the whole point. Whatever religion or philosophy of life you look at, nobody has come up with an explanation of suffering that makes total sense. We're all at sea, all baffled by the world we find ourselves in.

So rather than blaming, would you be interested in trying to understand just what might be going on? I know of an ancient piece of writing that makes some striking points on this topic. Let me describe its contents to you...

★ ★ ★

The story of Job
Two fascinating facts:

The book of Job (named after its main character) is one of the earliest books in the Bible.

It deals almost exclusively with the issue of suffering. (Seems our problem is one that has haunted humanity from the beginning of time!)

The story of Job has seven key players:

Job Wealthy, honest, generous, God-loving. The unknown author of the book goes so far as to use the word 'blameless'. Job is serious about serving God.

God Imperial, impartial... but thoroughly pleased with Job's integrity and devotion.

Satan A powerful angelic spirit. Envious, evil, and quick to find fault.

Job's four friends A well-meaning, but self-righteous and insensitive foursome. Though they turn up to support Job in his time of disaster, their 'help' makes his suffering even worse. (In fact, the term 'Job's Comforters' has come into the language to describe people who make you feel worse than you were to begin with!)

The story begins with a council in heaven. Satan is present. God points out to him the qualities of Job: 'a man who fears God and shuns evil'. Satan, keen to undermine Job's efforts, argues that his faith is strong only because he has everything to live for – health, wealth, family, respect, friends. Would Job obey and love you if he got nothing out of it? 'Take it all away,' says Satan, 'and Job will surely curse God.' Scene One ends with God agreeing to stand back. He will allow Satan to put Job to the test.

Scene two. Satan begins his programme of demoralisation. Without warning Job's whole world falls apart. First he hears that all his livestock have been captured by a raiding party of marauders and his servants killed. No sooner is this calamity announced than another messenger arrives with news that his children are dead. A freak storm has destroyed the house they were partying in.

Job is devastated. His children and all his worldly wealth gone in a single day. Yet despite his overwhelming grief he bows his head and acknowledges that 'the Lord gives and the Lord takes away'. He has no claim to preferential treatment by God.

Satan is furious – and vindictive. Back in heaven he now maintains that Job's loyalty to God is only skin deep. 'Suppose you hurt his body – he will curse you to your face.' God, scrupulously impartial (even with Satan), gives permission for Job to suffer. Satan proceeds to inflict on Job 'painful sores from the soles of his feet to the top of his head'. Covered with boils and still devastated by the loss of property and family, Job drags himself to the rubbish heap, takes a piece of broken pottery, and scrapes his sores. But even so he resists the temptation to self-pity or anger, accepting that misfortune is an inevitable consequence of the uncertainty of life.

His wife's faith is less robust. Distraught at the loss of her family and wealth, she urges Job to curse God and die. Act One finishes with Job sticking to his guns: 'When God sends us something good, we welcome it. How can we complain when he sends us trouble?'

In Act Two Job's friends arrive on the scene. They've heard about the calamities and are eager to help their neighbour. But when they see him they are appalled. So severe is his disease that they hardly recognise him. Overcome at the sight of their friend's suffering, and at a loss for words, they sit with him in embarrassed silence.

Finally it is Job who speaks. Despite his attempts to accept his fate, he's human and in pain. 'I have no peace, no rest, and my troubles never end.' His friends respond with what they would like to think is helpful counsel. Eliphaz is the first. He begins with kindly words but quickly moves to what he sees as the nub of the matter – 'Those who plough evil and those who sow trouble, reap it.' The source of all this suffering must be something that Job himself has done.

Job is shattered. He has lost everything – and now his friend tells him it serves him right! He knows that his heart's longing is to live for God. That he has never done anything to offend God. What sort of justice is it when the harder you try the worse you suffer? What sort of friends add to your pain by blaming you for everything? 'You've gone too far. Don't condemn me. I've only ever done what's right.'

But this is more than his friends can accept. They reprimand Job for his arrogance. 'If you are so honest and pure, then God will come and help you.' If God doesn't act to save him... obviously Job is at fault. That's the end of the matter.

Completely misunderstood, Job tries to defend himself. But for every argument he offers, his uncaring friends produce a counter accusation. At last Job is overwhelmed by the injustice of it all. Finally he cries out against God himself. 'You are treating me cruelly... Why do you attack a ruined man?'

Now Job's friends are really outraged. Convinced that suffering is God's punishment for sin, they pour more and more guilt on Job's head. Instead of comfort, love and support, he is given a series of lectures!

Poor Job is crushed. It's all gone so hopelessly wrong. 'I call to you, God, but you never answer. When I pray you pay no attention... Why do you attack a ruined man?'

Suddenly God does answer! In a dramatic finale he bursts into the debate. Speaking through a storm God ignores the self-righteous friends and goes straight to Job. 'Brace yourself like a man; I will question you, and you shall answer me. Where were you when I laid the earth's foundations?' The tables are turned. God – the one we all like to blame for pain and suffering – becomes the accuser! 'Where were you,' he thunders, 'when I made this universe? What do you know about the way it functions?'

Job is silenced. He has no choice but to admit his ignorance. 'I know that you can do all things,' he whispers. 'No plan of yours can be thwarted... Surely I spoke of things I did not understand, things too wonderful for me to know.'

But God isn't here to kick a man when he's down. Job may never know what caused all his misery, but God now intends to put it right. First, some straight talking to his so-called friends. 'I'm angry with you. You didn't speak the truth about me, as my servant Job did.' He orders them to apologise to Job – who, he says, will pray for them. 'And I will answer his prayer and not disgrace you as you deserve.'

And now he turns his attention to Satan's schemes. The whole miserable affair is overthrown. Job recovers his health, his farm prospers beyond anything he's known before, and his wife gives birth to seven sons and three gorgeous daughters. (The daughters, says our author, turn Job into a doting father!)

When the curtain finally falls, Job has lived to a ripe old age, richly blessed by God, seeing and enjoying not only his grandchildren, but even his great-grandchildren.

* * *

The lessons of Job

The story of Job gives a whole new perspective on the question of evil and suffering – and yet, believe it or not, nowhere does it provide an answer to the 'Why' question! Instead, it rebukes those who give only simplistic explanations. Job's comforters are condemned for trivialising his pain.

More than anything else, Job's story teaches us that God is way ahead of us on this matter. Our human complaints are left looking small and inadequate. The clear message is this: despite all that we cannot explain, there is a loving God who has our best interests at heart at all times, and who calls us to trust him when things don't work out.

The book of Job is a story of mystery and of faith. Only when all possible explanations of his misery are dismissed as unreasonable does Job at last come to terms with the enigma that is suffering. A writer by the name of Mike Mason (in his book *The Gospel According to Job*, Crossway Books, 1994) puts it this way:

There is a strange thing that happens at the point where we finally, somehow, manage to give up wrestling with matters that are too complex, too lofty, too wonderful for the human mind to understand. What happens is... suddenly, inexplicably, we do understand! For there is a knowledge that is beyond mere knowing.

At this moment of 'knowing', Job finds a new, deeper faith in God. He has no answers to what he has experienced, but he is ready to trust the one who not only has the answers but who also holds the future in his hands.

8: No easy ride

 Suffering can make us either a better or a bitter person.

There's a term that missionaries use: 'rice Christians'. These are people who apparently convert to Christianity – yet their real motivation is their desire to be looked after by the missionaries, given food and money and special treatment. Yet the truth of the matter seems to be that if you seriously set out to follow God, you could end up suffering *more*, not less.

Jesus himself went out of his way to help anyone he met who was suffering. Those, like myself, who genuinely make him our model, may well find ourselves caring for hurting people. Indeed, I fear the truth is even more ominous. Jesus chose to bear the pain of others, to take it on his own head. There is no guarantee that his followers won't also end up suffering deeply.

It may not come to that. But even in the ordinary routines of life, people who call themselves Christians are not given any promise of an easy ride. There are no rice Christians! Becoming a follower of Jesus is no insurance for avoiding the disasters that seem to settle haphazardly on us humans. It was Jesus, after all, who said, *He (God) gives his best – the sun to warm and the rain to nourish – to everyone, regardless: the good and bad, the nice and nasty* (Matthew 5:45).

One of the striking things about Job is that he really struggled to be the sort of person God wanted him to be. Yet everything in his world suddenly fell apart. And for no understandable reason. It's a dilemma that is not limited to ancient books! I've seen it happen among my own friends. The experience of Viv and Trevor brought it home to me in a heart-breaking way.

★ ★ ★

An anatomy of grief

'See ya later, buddy,' Viv whispered to her five-year-old son Jared as she pulled up outside school. Jared wheeled around momentarily to give Viv a squeeze and to kiss Janelle, his ten-week-old baby sister, on the cheek. Then he was off.

'Have a good day!'

It was a warm, late summer morning. Viv's son had been at school little more than three weeks, and he was loving it. Jared, a boy with endless energy and a broad beaming smile, was giving school everything he had.

Around lunchtime that same day, the phone rang in the Salisbury household. It was the school. The conversation was short and to the point. 'Could you please come down? Jared's had an accident. He was playing on the jungle gym and fell off. He's okay, but he's just fallen asleep.'

A thousand thoughts raced through Viv's mind. Being a teacher herself she knew that when a child gets hurt at school you ring the parents when it's more than just first aid stuff.

'But I thought to myself, "It's okay, he's probably been concussed and just fallen asleep," as many kids do when they've had a fall. Jared was always doing silly things, so it was probably about time he had an accident! I mean, he would clamber out of windows, he would climb up trees and fall out of them. As a toddler he always had a row of bruises across his forehead and down his shins. And if he didn't you'd think, "What's missing?"'

The jumbled, anxious thoughts were cut short by Viv's need to get to the school. She called out to her husband Trevor who was working in his office upstairs. Then she rang Trevor's mother who lived next door, explaining the situation and asking her to look after Janelle for them.

At the school the small sick bay was full of adults. Jared was lying on the bed, unconscious. A couple of teachers automatically moved aside to let Trevor and Viv see their son. The small, still frame looked a picture of serenity, but they knew straight away that he was not okay. Far from it. Trevor and Viv instinctively began to pray for their boy, asking God to take control of the situation and to look after him.

An ambulance was already on its way. The school had acted quickly and had called the doctor from the medical centre across the road. Taking one look at Jared, he knew it was serious. He'd been part of a hospital neurological team himself, so he immediately alerted the neurological staff at Wellington Hospital – 30 minutes away by road. A helicopter had been considered, but it was decided that enough could be done to stabilise Jared in the ambulance.

At the entrance to the hospital the neurological team were ready and waiting. Jared was whisked away quickly, initially for a brain scan and then to the operating theatre. The doctor's diagnosis had been correct. It was a blood clot, and Trevor and Viv were assured that it was a fairly routine piece of brain surgery.

Nevertheless, the waiting seemed interminable. Assuring themselves that it shouldn't take too much longer, the Salisburys continued to pray that God would heal their little boy. A song they'd been singing at church the Sunday before buzzed through their minds. The 'battle' did belong to God, just as the words said. They were convinced he was in control. A progress report from the charge nurse was less encouraging. She took Trevor and Viv into an office and said, 'This is actually a bit more serious than we first thought.'

Not long after, the surgeon entered the room. His look said it all. He was shattered. They had lost Jared.

The doctor fought back tears as he explained what had happened. The impact of the fall had jolted Jared's spine and caused a blood vessel to burst in his brain. The team had patched up the vessel but, just as they were finishing, some air got into the blood and down into the heart. He fought for over 30 minutes, but eventually his little heart gave out.

In the room with Trevor and Viv was the principal of the school. She broke down and wept.

Jared's body was brought through to the recovery room. The staff had cleaned him up and bandaged his head. Trevor and Viv touched and stroked him. He was still warm.

Even now, it's difficult for the couple to think about the implications of that moment. Says Viv, 'It was all just like a dream. It wasn't really happening. I think that's why you manage to keep going – like in shock. It's just a dream that you're going to wake up from. But the longer it went on the more I realised that Jared wasn't going to wake up. This was it.'

Trevor felt the same. 'I remember on the way home in the car saying to whoever was with me, "I feel like I've just gone 12 rounds with Mike Tyson." I felt very weak – emotionally, physically and spiritually whacked. But the hurt and the loss still hadn't sunk in. It took weeks and months for that.'

In the midst of the tragedy some decisions had to be made. Trevor and Viv decided that to help them come to terms with things, they would have Jared home until the funeral. An autopsy had to be done first, but then a friend who was a funeral director organised everything.

In the days leading up to the funeral, the Salisbury home was alive with people.

'We didn't realise how many good friends we had. No one knew what to say. I mean, what *could* you say? We must have had hundreds of people through the house over the next few days. Some wanted to see Jared and some just weren't ready for that.

He was 'lying in state' in the lounge. Some of Jared's school friends came up and brought little notes to tuck into the casket with him. Some of our Maori friends from church led waiatas (songs) and prayers. Different folk just kept coming in. We felt like we were in a florist shop!'

The day of the funeral is a bit of a blur for Trevor and Viv. A friend of theirs who had lost his teenage son some years earlier spoke, and many others shared their memories of the little boy with the infectious smile.

* * *

Meaning in grief?

When you talk to Trevor and Viv it's clear that there were never any regrets about Jared, no sense of 'I should have done this or that'. Their faith in God had led them to pray for him every day, and the memories remained of five full and rewarding years.

Yet still there is the inevitable pain. Trevor says it hits him in funny places – like one time in a doctor's waiting room where he saw a magazine. One of the photos showed a father fishing with his son.

Looking back, they both see how in many ways God prepared them for the pain and trauma of losing their child. Trevor recalls: 'I remember once hearing a friend talk about losing his teenage son. At the time I really felt challenged quite clearly, "What would *my* response be if this happened to *me*?" Whether it was just my own mind asking the question or whether it was God, I don't know, but I certainly faced it. I didn't just shrug it off. It came back to me about two months before Jared's death. I was in the shower once when it really hit me. I cried and cried.

'When I was following the ambulance into Wellington, I just knew it was all over. There was something in my heart which said, "Lord, this is it, isn't it?"

'There were other things which prepared me too. For instance, I don't know why, but for the 18 months before Jared's death I felt the need to get up early to pray and read the Bible. Sometimes I didn't get heaps out of it but I was very disciplined in the time I spent with God. Then after Jared's death I found that I really couldn't talk to God much. It wasn't because I was angry with him, or bitter. I was just speechless. I didn't have anything to say. But in that period I remembered the times with God in the months before Jared's death. I think they acted as a bit of a reservoir, a resource to get me through.

'I believe God prepared me spiritually for that time. He's a bit like an engineer. When an engineer puts a steel beam to the test to see whether it can take the stress and weight, he is pretty confident that it's going to handle the pressure. I think that's a bit like what happened with me. God had the confidence that I could handle the pressure he allowed to be put on my life, because of the groundwork in my relationship with him. Of course, that didn't make it any easier emotionally, but it did make it a lot easier spiritually.'

Grief expanded

The death of their son Jared was not the first tragedy the Salisburys had experienced. Neither was it to be their last.

Some years before, while returning from Palmerston North late one night Trevor had had a serious car accident. Apart from the trauma, and the eight months on crutches, the head-on collision had some major implications for Trevor and his future. A builder by trade, he was forced to change his work. A shattered ankle brought very limited mobility, particularly on uneven surfaces. This meant that he could no longer work on a building site. In his early thirties, he found himself forced into a management role.

At the time of Jared's death, things were not going well in the business. High borrowings and a major slump in the property market had caused real difficulties. And then a major investor client went broke. Reeling from the loss of his son, Trevor found himself in financial turmoil as he tried to keep his business afloat.

'Just a couple of weeks after Jared died, I remember going onto a building site one day and hitting my head against a wall and saying, "What the hell am I going through this for?" I was trying to make decisions at a time when I just couldn't handle them.'

Trevor and Viv determined to do everything within their power to keep the business going so as to avoid owing money to creditors. To produce more finance they resolved to sell their home. Viv remembers well the day they moved house.

'It was Trevor's fortieth birthday. Forty tends to be an age where every guy checks where he's got to in life. It's a real watershed for many. And there we were having to shift out of our home! There was no thought of celebration.

'Trevor came in as I was struggling to finish cleaning. We were leaving this lovely house that I had put my whole self into. I was worn out, coping with the need to move and under a lot of strain – it was only eight months after Jared died. Trevor offered to help me clean up and I told him, "No, you don't do it well enough. I've got to do it." The next minute I realised he had disappeared.

'Then I had a dreadful thought. "Have I pushed him over the edge?" I guess I panicked. I mean, I wasn't thinking straight. I was really worried. I drove down to the river to see if he was there. It was where he would often go for a time of quiet. There was no sign of him. Finally, some time later I found him. When I told him how concerned I'd been that he would kill himself, he said to me, "Oh don't be so ridiculous. I wouldn't do anything like that!"'

Maybe not – but Trevor's business was in a bad way, and getting worse.

'At times when things were getting extremely difficult and it was looking like there was no way out, I would sometimes go up to Jared's graveside for a time of reflection. I remember this particular day. It had been raining. The grass was wet and they had just cut down a whole block of pine trees, some of which were very close to the row of graves where Jared was. All that was left were the stumps. I remembered a verse in the Bible that in essence asks the question, "When the tree is cut down and only the stump remains, will new life come, will it grow again?" That hit me. My life was being reduced to a stump. I just lay on the ground and I cried and cried.'

Within a few months of his son's death, it became obvious that the business was going to collapse. Liquidation came first, but worse was to follow. Trevor's solicitor had given him advice that was detrimental to the business and to Trevor's family. Unnecessary transactions took place that may have protected the solicitor but were not in the family's interest. Substantial tax claims were incurred for which Trevor and his family were liable. Negotiations with the authorities were attempted. Now came the crushing news that those negotiations had failed. This was the final disaster. It left only one option. Trevor was declared bankrupt.

Yet even then the struggle wasn't over. At the time of Jared's death other members of Trevor and Viv's family had put their own financial security on the line. In their commitment as a close-knit family they wanted to help as much as possible and responsibly manage the growing crisis. With the authorities immovable, they were backed into a corner. About a month after negotiations broke down, Trevor accompanied his father and brother-in-law into the High Court, where they filed for voluntary bankruptcy. This was the hardest thing he had ever done. Son, home, business, financial independence and family money – all lost in a period of some 24 months.

And yet there was more that was lost as well. Viv explains: 'Not only was the death of our son devastating, but added to that was the loss of our home, business and reputation and the overwhelming impact on the family. And in many ways, because of what Trevor was working through, I felt I had lost my husband as well. Life always used to be fun with Trevor and if I didn't have a good laugh every day I knew there was something wrong. But then we went through patches where there was no fun; just struggle and tears.

'On top of it all, to know that we had affected our family in the same way, and forced them to cope with bankruptcy and the loss of their homes and savings – that was the hardest thing of all.

'The grief with Jared was clean. Everyone had done all they possibly could to keep him alive. The school had, the surgeon and his team had. There was no one you could pin any blame on. With Jared everything was out of our hands. But in the case of our business we had some degree of responsibility. So it was very different to the grief of Jared's death.'

Crushing despair

That was what brought a crushing sense of despair to Trevor as well. He felt a deep responsibility for the extra stress the bankruptcy had caused Viv, to say nothing of his parents, sister and brother-in-law.

But there were other factors involved involved. 'About that time, one night I walked again along the route I used to take as a kid to school. I was actually supposed to be at a meeting that night, but it was the last place I wanted to be, so I didn't go. Parking the car not far from where we used to live, I walked to school, past the same houses and fences I used to walk past decades earlier. The trees had grown about 20 feet higher but most things seemed the same.

'Then I sat down on the seats that I used to have lunch on as a five- or six-year-old. It was a bright moonlit night and I looked out over the field and the same playground.

'I was re-living my life as my boy Jared did in his few days at school. As I sat there, for a split second I felt the loneliest person in the whole universe. I felt there was no one there but me, as though I had neither a past nor a future. I had really lost a lot of the past – particularly financially and what had happened with the family. And because of Jared, I didn't feel like I had a future either.'

Is God fair?

Well, is he? Both Trevor and Viv acknowledge that at times it has been hard for them to reconcile what they have experienced with what they know in their hearts – that the God they follow is just and fair.

'One of the things that made it so hard with the business,' says Viv, 'was knowing that at any time God could just click his fingers and deal with the problem. We prayed and did everything "right" – everything that was supposed to be the right "formula" to "make God work".

'We believed in a just God – but it didn't seem fair. It felt like we'd taken everyone else's hassles. I mean, why couldn't he just share them around? It got to the stage where you wondered what was going to happen next. You'd feel a lump so you'd automatically expect it to be cancer. I didn't want to get bitter, but I often thought, "Why don't you pick on someone else for a change, God?"'

Trevor nods. 'Sometimes I would think, "Well, God's got to be consistent." Someone will get up in church and say how much they are thankful that God has healed them of cancer. Then a few weeks later someone else shares that a friend's wife has only six months to live. You get to the stage of saying, "God, what's the story here? You can't expect to take the credit for the good things and not expect to take the blame for the bad things! God, let's be real." So I started to question my concept of God.'

Viv adds, 'So did I. My idea of God had to change. I found that the little box I had built for him wouldn't fit any longer. I had to change the whole way I viewed him. That's what was so hard. In fact, it was shattering. I thought I knew God – but the truth was that I didn't. When God was in my little box, playing by my rules, I was in control. But when I opened up the box and saw that God is who he is and won't be restricted to my rules, I lost control.'

The forever factor

For me, chatting with Trevor and Viv was a sobering affair. They're at pains to point out they haven't got it all 'sussed'. Yet there's a strong thread of hope woven through all they say. Something that causes them to believe we're made for more than just this life. They call it 'the forever factor' – the idea that there's more than just this world. They're convinced that belief in an afterlife not only helps them come to terms with Jared's brief life; it will also ultimately explain what now seems inexplicable.

Trevor told me how, since Jared's death, he's noticed the reactions of people at funerals. What has struck him is the two-edged sword of grief – not only the pain of loss, but also the gripping awareness of one's own mortality. Often it's only the heightened pain of grief, he says, that can bring such a reality check. The awareness that one day this is going to be me. That there has to be more than just this life.

Viv and Trevor have changed. They've come to see other perspectives on their own painful experiences. One of their insights is learning to distinguish between the two statements 'God isn't fair' and 'Life isn't fair'. They're not the same. In fact, according to the Salisburys, God has been incredibly generous to them despite the unfairness of life. Our natural tendency to blame God for everything that goes sour is itself… unfair. Perhaps this is what has freed them from becoming bitter and twisted. In fact, you can sense that they've not just survived the hard times, they've *grown* through them. Even though their lives have fallen to pieces, their world has fallen apart, a process of rebuilding has been set in motion. There's an increasing strength that wasn't there before.

Says Trevor, 'We'll never know all the answers to life but at the end of the day it's about trusting God. The issue is relationship, not knowledge. There's an old saying, "When the heart is content, the mind is satisfied." That's certainly true for us. In fact, if you take God out of the picture, life makes even less sense.'

A reason for the unreasonable?

You and I are searching for reasons, trying to understand why people suffer. It's an important search, and I've invested years of my life in it. That's why I'm writing this book, after all! I've done it believing that finding some answers – even if they're patently not the *whole* answer – is important.

But along the way I have learned something else too. I've learned, from the story of Job and from the experience of the

Salisburys, that when you're looking at individuals and their pain, the very process of searching for a reason can be a brutal act. To put their lives under the microscope while you try to work out why this happened to *them*, rather than to some other person less worthy... that can be cruel. That can be rubbing sandpaper on their wound. That's holding up a camera to their moment of misery and saying, 'Come and look, everybody. Let's find out what's wrong with these people!'

Nobody deserves that sort of cruelty, least of all those who have been bitterly hurt. Nobody deserves to have their time of pain exposed to the world and minutely dissected. In suffering, our friends need compassion – not surgical incisions. After all our wise questions, even if we do produce some sort of learned explanation, what does it change for them?

When it comes to the disasters that we as individuals find ourselves caught up in, hunting for *reasons* can easily take us to a dead-end street. At those times, says writer Mike Mason (*The Gospel According to Job*, Crossway Books, 1994), something else – something very different – is happening:

In every season of suffering there comes a turning point. The turning point is not usually the point at which the suffering itself is alleviated. Rather, it is that time when it begins to dawn upon the sufferer that there may actually be a meaning to his pain.

When we stop looking for causes or reasons, when we instead ask ourselves, 'What has happened to *me* through this?'... or, 'How is my world different because of this?'... then at last something changes within us.

Not finding *a reason for it*... but *a meaning within it*.

This is no easy step. We're all good at wallowing in self-pity and focusing on our sad state, but to put that aside and to discover how suffering might be an opportunity for learning and growth – now there's a challenge, as the story of Job illustrates, and as Viv and Trevor found.

After all their pain, they may not necessarily be able to understand one single jot more about why they've gone through this mess, but because of all the sadness and loss they've certainly discovered more about themselves, more about the God they follow, more about the world he has put them in, and more about the people they share that world with.

Dare I say... ?

So perhaps we may (very cautiously) say this much: suffering can be, as writer and theologian C S Lewis has put it, God's megaphone. His way of getting our attention. His way of getting us off the roundabout of self-centredness. Often we become far more receptive to what he wants to do in our lives when we experience pain or are in the midst of suffering.

Why am I treading so gingerly when I say this? Well, I'm conscious of what a hornets' nest I'm holding! You see, the trouble with this whole topic of suffering is that it's fiercely complicated. So let me protect myself from at least two hornet stings...

★ I'm not suggesting that everyone who suffers becomes more open to God. Far from it. Often it has the opposite effect, hardening a person and producing bitterness rather than receptivity.

★ I'm not saying that God brings suffering just so that we'll listen to him. We blame God for all sorts of things, but it would be monstrous to suggest he devises tortures and cruelty in order to further his purposes.

The point I'm making is simply this: suffering and pain – natural parts of life here on earth – are frequently great opportunities for us to grow. On the one hand, they lead us to new perspectives about what is important in life; and on the other, they keep us from getting inflated ideas about our own immortality.

And one more disclaimer. I've said that God makes use of the suffering we go through. When I acknowledge this, I am not suggesting that it makes the hurt easier to bear. You can't just magic away pain! But something happens to that pain when we see it being turned to a positive purpose. Women often say it's like this with childbirth. The memory of the pain is swamped by the miracle of new life that it brings. In the same way, when God uses suffering to bring growth in our lives the whole issue moves into a completely different dimension.

Maybe of all God's miracles this is his greatest – to turn tears to joy, to bring a positive result out of what seems to be wholly negative.

There, I've extricated myself from as much trouble as I can. Now if only I could be as precise about exactly *how* it is that suffering changes us! But I can't. Perhaps we never will be able to. All I know is that through it we can grow. We can become more mature and complete than we were before the bad times came.

And the bad times *will* come! They do to every one of us. At some time in your life you will wake to find that you stand alone, facing hurt that seems beyond bearing. What you will become, the sort of person you will be, the character that you will take into the rest of your life… is determined by how you respond to that suffering. Will it ultimately make you a better or a bitter person?

 Bless you, prison… for it was in you that I discovered that the meaning of earthly existence lies, not as we have grown used to thinking, in prospering, but in the development of the soul.
Alexander Solzhenitsyn

9: The suffering God

We've been searching for answers to the age-old question. I hope you agree we've made at least *some* progress. If nothing else, the problem is getting clearer!

But I freely admit... we haven't come up with a full and satisfying answer. We have a dilemma here that goes to the very root of what it means to be human – and we're baffled by it! The truth is, it seems, we're dealing with a sickness that is so deeply a part of our lives and our world that we're trapped in the middle of the mystery. We can't separate ourselves from it.

The only possible way to make any sense of our predicament is to step outside the universe... to stand apart from it so that we'll be able to see it in total. I suppose what I'm saying is, we would have to be God to comprehend it all. Maybe when we die and go to be with him, then finally we'll see it with his eyes. Then we'll understand.

That's fine, and I look forward to the time when I at last see clearly. But the trouble is... that does little to help me, here and now, with the cruelty I both experience and cause.

What would really help? Well, if only, at my times of greatest pain, there was someone who not only understands but who would also live this life with me, someone who knows what it's like and who will stand alongside me as I battle with my times of pain... someone who has seen it and understood it from God's perspective... and who has lived it in mine!

In all of history one person *has* laid claim to both views. One person has grappled with the problem from both sides. As best I can tell, there is just one fellow-sufferer who holds the keys to our problem. That person is the most significant figure in all of history. The one who has had more impact on the life of this planet than any other.

I am, of course, talking about Jesus Christ.

The Palestine prophet

So, who is this man Jesus that we Christians say was God? And what claim does he have to speak authoritatively on the problem of our human suffering?

* * *

Jesus Christ was born around 4 BC into a poor Jewish family, in a period of political turbulence. The Jews were at the time under the domination of the great Roman empire – a fact of bitter resentment to many. Life for most was hard and uncertain.

Not much is known about his childhood, but at around the age of 30 Jesus embarked on an itinerant lifestyle in and around Palestine, taking with him a group of men and women from a wide range of backgrounds. Wherever he travelled Jesus spoke about God's heart for all people, but particularly for the despised and downtrodden.

Huge crowds flocked to hear him speak and see him heal. He was a master storyteller and used his skills to explain who God is and what God wants to do in this world of his. People responded to this message of love and peace. Jesus offered them dignity and value – and a future filled with hope.

And though he talked a lot about this future, he was also serious about the problems of people in the here and now. When he met those who were suffering from sickness and disease, he didn't simply console them with talk of a perfect life in the next world. Far from it. He made it his concern to deal with their immediate pain. If they were sick, he healed them. If they were hungry, he fed them. Even down to what we might consider trivial problems:

in one celebrated incident he produced a miraculous supply of wine for an embarrassed bridal couple at their wedding feast.

But, here's the important point. He never pretended that these earthbound miracles were the full answer. They were, he explained, signs to the future – that future where one day pain and suffering would be no more.

Needless to say, Jesus gained a growing reputation for his miraculous healings. But he himself downplayed them. They were not central to what he was about. For him the key was helping people to live the full and rich life that comes from following God.

And this man seemed to 'walk the talk'. His miracles won him fame, of course. But it was his genuine care and love that blew people's minds.

Yet not everyone was happy. Some of what he did and said raised hackles among his listeners. On one occasion – it was in the neighbourhood where he grew up – Jesus hinted that he was more than just a man. His hearers, including no doubt many who knew him as a child and a youth, were shocked at what they saw as blasphemy. In the uproar that followed Jesus was almost stoned to death. He escaped by mysteriously disappearing from the middle of the riot.

But it wasn't long before this miracle-working Jew began to attract attention from the authorities. They were concerned about his growing influence. For much of the last two years of his life Jesus lived with constant veiled threats from the Jewish religious leaders. Running scared, they were ready to conspire and manipulate in order to deal with this challenge to their own power base. Unimpressed by his message of peace and love, they looked for an opportunity to eliminate Jesus. They calculated that their Roman masters would play along with the plan in order to quell any potential uprising – something that the Roman governor of the time was only too willing to do.

The worst kind of betrayal

Enter Judas Iscariot. For over two years Judas had followed the man he believed would liberate the Jewish nation from their Roman oppressors. He wasn't alone in this hope. We know that others, in his close group of followers and outside it, had grand ideas of how Jesus might lead a revolt from Rome, how he might wage a successful war and give back to the Jews their ancient independence.

To his credit, Judas had given his all for the cause. He'd left his home and family and job to join the band of Jesus' followers. He held a responsible position among them – as their treasurer he was accountable for the money the group had to live on.

Though Judas was a close friend of Jesus, gradually it became clear that the disciple and the teacher had very different views on how to improve the lot of their people. Judas's betrayal of him to the authorities, when it came, was no surprise to Jesus, but it must nevertheless have been a cruel blow. Judas, too, when he saw the results of his actions, was appalled. He was so shattered that he hanged himself.

Abandoned

If Judas was a traitor, what about the other close companions of Jesus? The truth is, they were demoralised by the turn of events. Though, like Peter, they fiercely declared their intention of standing by Jesus whatever happened, at the moment of crisis their loyalty crumbled. When Jesus was arrested they panicked and ran. Fearing recognition Peter swore – three times – that he had no connection with Jesus.

The crowds too deserted Jesus. Prior to his arrest he had entered Jerusalem in something akin to a ticker-tape parade. He was hailed as hero and liberator. Yet within a week the same people turned on him, baying for his blood and opting to have a murderer released from prison, rather than the man they had so recently idolised.

During his trial and execution, Jesus was bereft of support. The fickle crowd, his followers and even most of his closest friends no longer stuck with him. He was left to face the music by himself.

Death by torture

Arrested on trumped-up charges, Jesus faced an extended and humiliating trial that lasted through the night. It was followed by immediate punishment for his 'crime'.

A Roman execution was routinely carried out in such a way that death, when it finally came, was a longed-for release. First, Jesus was subjected to a brutal flogging. The usual method was to strip the victim bare and tie him to a post. Several soldiers would then use a whip whose leather thongs were fitted with pieces of bone or lead. With each lash these studs would catch the skin and rip deep. By the end of the flogging, the victim would be a bloodied mess of torn flesh. Bones would be exposed; sometimes even entrails. Small wonder that Jesus needed help to carry the heavy crossbeam on the way to his place of execution.

Crucifixion is one of the most cruel methods of capital punishment ever devised. It was reasonably common in the days of Jesus but was reserved only for those who were not Roman citizens. One of the privileges of citizenship was to be spared this agonising death. It was, therefore, a brutally effective tool for restraining rebellion – especially in unruly areas like Palestine. One Roman commander used mass crucifixions to terrify Jews with the consequences of sedition.

Death on a cross was a long, excruciating affair. It could sometimes take several days of unrelenting torture. Hanging naked by his arms from the crossbar, the victim found his lungs constricted. To snatch a breath he had to push himself up by his feet. As the hours wore on, this exhausting procedure became harder and harder, until eventually the poor wretch died of asphyxiation, unable to gasp in enough air to breathe. Sometimes, in order to speed up the process, a soldier would break the condemned man's legs. This meant that it was no longer possible for him to push his exhausted body upwards to catch even the shortest of breaths.

Because the Jewish authorities wanted the execution site cleared before the Passover festival began, at the end of the afternoon soldiers went to break the legs of the three men who were being executed that day. They were surprised, when they came to Jesus, to find that he had already died.

The nightmare was finally over.

The pain of God

Don Carson writes (in *How Long, O Lord?*, Baker Books 1990):

If anyone knows what suffering is like, God does. The humiliating and painful death Jesus experienced was the last of a string of injustices dealt to him during his short life of 33 years. Jesus' wounds are his credentials.

If Jesus was God, as I believe, you cannot accuse him of being insulated or removed from our suffering. Far from it. He too has suffered deeply. What's more, it seems clear his torture and murder were totally undeserved. He was blameless.

Writer Philip Yancey says, *God's only excuse is Easter*. He's right. Becoming human was the most loving response God could have made to the human dilemma of pain and suffering. He chose to leave aside his power and take the risk of this evil-infected and cruel world. It seems crazy in the light of day. Yet God did it because of his commitment to the human race... to the species he had himself designed with such care... to the creatures he persisted in loving through so many disasters.

Despite everything, that commitment that we've seen surface time and time again over the centuries led him to this incredible act... God as a man placed himself at the mercy of his created beings; letting them do what they wanted with him; and then God as a man died – utterly alone, crushed with suffering and pain.

In our own hurt and anger, we often get it wrong. God isn't like some grumpy schoolmaster bringing retribution and telling us to take our medicine. God knows we are caught up in a world we can't make sense of. To show his love, he shared our pain. He came right into the middle of it, to suffer just as we do – and far more than most of us will ever know.

10: Light from a dark star

The dark star is an enigma. A star with little or no visible light. Other evidence points to its existence, such as when it eclipses another star. Suffering, grief, pain... most times there's little illumination. No warmth, no certain light, no easy explanation. But still valuable, still part of the pattern and purpose of the universe.

The idea that God would identify so totally with his children is astonishing. It may be the warmest and most moving story in all of history. Each year at Easter millions of Christians re-live the wonder of it.

And yet...

And yet, if it was just a case of God identifying with our pain and experiencing it in the flesh himself, then the truth is, it doesn't change anything. He can have as much empathy with our fate as he wants to, but if he's powerless to do anything about it, what good does it do us in the end... ?

Worse still: some might say the cross is a sign of failure. A despairing sort of gesture. The captain going down with his ship. The end of a great dream. The final surrender. God admits defeat.

The little band of Jesus's followers must have felt something like that. For them the gut-wrenching experience of seeing their leader's limp body brought down from the cross and laid in a cave was effectively the end. The end of a roller-coaster three years, but, more important, the end of all real hope. Jesus had talked to them so much about liberation and the future, and he'd backed that up with a series of miracles and healings. But to all intents and purposes, those words and actions were now just memories.

A cosmic plan?

And yet... are we missing something here?

What *really* happened that day? Is there another of Jesus's miracles here, this time hidden behind the events? Was a battle being fought of which we see no more than fleeting glimpses?

If those despairing followers hadn't been so devastated by the disaster unfolding around them, perhaps they might have wondered at certain strange signs. And if they'd remembered earlier words of Jesus, perhaps they might have noticed that he was not as unnerved as they were. For death at the hands of the authorities was no unexpected shock to Jesus. In fact, he predicted it. And clearly he saw a purpose – dare I say it, a destiny – in his impending execution. How else can we explain some of the statements that Jesus made? Like...

> *The greatest way to show love for friends is to die for them.* John 15:13

> *I tell you for certain that a grain of wheat that falls on the ground will never be more than one grain unless it dies. But if it dies, it will produce lots of wheat.* John 12:24

Speaking of his own mission, Jesus claimed that he:

> *did not come to be a slave master, but a slave who will give his life to rescue many people...* Mark 10:45

If those followers had not been so thrown by events they might have begun to wonder, even at the blackest moment, that something unexpected was afoot.

Eerily, the blackness was literal! One writer describes how for the last three hours of Jesus's life, from noon until about three o'clock, the whole earth was plunged into darkness. Had they thought about it, those despairing followers might have discerned a gleam of light! Was this eclipse of the sun just a freak coincidence or did it signify something with huge ramifications?

As Jesus breathed his last, a huge earthquake split enormous rocks and even opened up graves. No wonder the captain of the Roman guard responsible for enforcing the crucifixion was scared to death. He reputedly said, 'This has to be the Son of God!'

What was going on? Surely all this was more than just one man dying. Something about the way the death of Jesus was reported hints that his demise had not just personal but cosmic implications.

Breakthrough!

The physical pain was, for sure, horrific. And Jesus never pretended that it was anything other than frightening. But, as a human who was also God, he went through something else here, something even worse than the hours of bloody torture. When he said, in effect, 'My Father, if there is any way, get me out of this'; when he sweated blood; when he cried out on the cross, 'My God, My God, why have you abandoned me?'... something appalled him that was far more than the brutality unleashed on his body.

The writers of the New Testament reveal what was happening that day. In passage after passage they describe how Jesus went to his death carrying – alone – the full weight of the world's pain and evil.

When he faced his fate, they tell us, Jesus knew that he was about to do something beyond the guessing of anyone present. He understood only too well that in his death he was about to rescue the creatures he and his Father had made. He knew that he was taking on his own shoulders all the misery and horror of every person who would ever live.

For when Jesus went to his death he was not simply *identifying* with the sad and wounded inhabitants of this planet – incredible as that might be. He was also doing something much, much more far-reaching. That first Easter, God displayed not only a commitment to join his beleaguered creatures, but also a commitment to offer them *a future in which there would be no more suffering and pain*.

Those disciples in disarray were not to know, but the hope-shattering black day we now remember as Good Friday was the seed for the most hope-full day in human history. The early Christian writer Matthew describes what happened next:

After the Sabbath, as the first light of the new week dawned, Mary Magdalene and the other Mary came to keep vigil at the tomb. Suddenly the earth reeled and rocked under their feet as God's angel came down from Heaven, came right up to where they were standing. He rolled back the stone and then sat on it. Shafts of lightning blazed from him. His garments shimmered snow-white. The guards at the tomb were scared to death. They were so frightened, they couldn't move.

The angel spoke to the women, 'There is nothing to fear here. I know you're looking for Jesus, the One they nailed to the cross. He is not here. He was raised, just as he said. Come and look at the place where he was placed.

'Now, get on your way quickly and tell his disciples, "He is risen from the dead. He is going on ahead of you to Galilee. You will see him there." That's the message.'   Matthew 28:1–7

Like millions of others, I'm convinced that Jesus changed history when he was cruelly and publicly executed on that Friday. And my confidence stems from what happened to Jesus *after* he died. On Sunday morning everything changed. Suddenly, unexpectedly, astonishingly, God was in control! Jesus was not dead at all. He was thrillingly alive...

And he obviously had a plan and a purpose.

That much is clear, even if the full extent of that plan is beyond us. Though we still can't tie down neatly in words just how he has dealt with the question of pain and suffering, yet we see, like the dawning of a new day, the glimmering of a new hope. Even though we can't comprehend how we will be saved from ourselves, God can. The suffering will not be wasted. He has the will and the wisdom to turn our tears to laughter.

The greatest way to show love for friends is to die for them

How then do we put all this together? What does it mean for our attempt to understand the twisted world of suffering that you and I live in? Think back to the catalogue of violence I listed in Chapter 2, the awful account of 'man's inhumanity to man'. Now think of Jesus shouldering all that pain on a black Friday 2000 years ago.

Then add every unrecorded resentment and hatred and viciousness that every human has ever unleashed on another. All the pettiness of our behaviour down through the centuries and the millennia. All the grubbiness that a sad and bitter species has been able to concoct in its meanest and most warped thinking.

Include *your* worst moments... and mine.

All this Jesus took on his shoulders during those tortured hours. The cosmic implications of his supreme act of sacrifice were hidden from his followers that Friday. But they were dramatically revealed three days later – when Jesus cast aside the shackles of death and returned to life. To the astonishment even of those who knew him best, he broke through the age-old blockage that had trapped us humans in our bitter world of suffering. Jesus defeated death!

And there, in the One who died and now lives again, is a glimpse of what lies in store for us. A life of victory over the suffering and the death that dogs us here in this universe.

A signpost to the future

I have no doubt that a miracle of extraordinary proportions occurred that first Easter. What I find more difficult to explain is how it changes my situation in the here and now. It shouldn't come as any surprise that the answer to this is not simple or easy. We've already discovered how complex this issue of suffering is. Here is another tantalising angle on it...

The raising of Jesus from the dead was a sign (and indeed the beginning) of things to come. The body that his friends then saw and touched, the resurrected body of Jesus, was by all accounts very different from his pre-death one. It was permanent, not restricted by time and space, and unable to be racked by sickness and disease.

It was as if God was saying, *This present existence, full of pain and sorrow will one day come to an end, and a life more enduring and free of suffering will replace it. And even now this same power I used to raise Jesus from the dead is available to make a difference in the midst of your pain.*

This points to a very different future for us. Remember Viv and Trevor's 'forever factor'? One of the things God offers is the prospect of new life where there will be no tears. One day pain and suffering and death will perish. They will be no more. The Bible calls it heaven – an eternity when wrongs will be put right, when all will be made new. Never again will pain and suffering be possible.

Of course, many people assume that only what they can feel, hear and see is real. For them the idea of heaven is mere 'pie-in-the-sky' talk; a desperate belief in the midst of despair that death is not the end and that life's wrongs will be put right. To be sure, such a belief does give strength in times of pain. It's little wonder that Negroes in America sang and talked so much about heaven. In the midst of slavery and a hopeless future, it was the only hope they could cling to.

But that doesn't make it the easy option. In the ordinary ups and downs of life that most of us go through, believing in a heaven calls for a strong faith. Jesus knew that. Just before his arrest and violent death, he assured his closest followers that even though the next few days would bring anguish and confusion, things would be different on the other side of the grave.

Don't let this throw you (he said to them). *You trust in God, don't you? Trust me. There is plenty of room for you in my*

*Father's home. If that weren't so, would I have told you that I'm
on my way to get a room ready for you?*   John 14:1,2

From the way he talked, Jesus made it very clear that when this
world comes to an end, God will act to set all wrongs right. In
other words, while we may feel that evil people prosper in this
life and actually get away with it, ultimately God will have the
last say. All of us will be judged according to how we have lived.
Justice will reign supreme. No longer will there be unfairness.
No more will we have cause to cry out, 'Why me, God? It's just
not fair!'

I don't want to waste my time (or yours) guessing at the details
of the future. Whatever it is that God has in store for us, the
important thing is that when we are in the midst of suffering, we
haven't heard the final word. Knowing that life will continue
beyond the grave can give us strength to face the pain and suffering this side of death's door. And it can do more. It can help
us with the assurance that how we live in this present life will
ultimately count for something.

11: Agents for change

You'll remember that back in Chapter 3, I came to an uncomfortable conclusion – that as much as we are all victims of pain, we are also the cause of hurt to others. *We* are part of the problem. If we're to change that, to become, instead, part of the answer, then we must allow God to change *us*. We need him to heal our ugly side, the part of us that repeatedly hurts others in small and large ways. The same God who raised Jesus from the dead is capable of transforming us – if we allow him to.

If that sounds far-reaching, it's only part of the miracle. The next step in God's cosmic solution is that he will then use *us* to alleviate the pain and suffering in the world. We will become his partners in working to relieve the anguish of others.

What one person *can* do

I often have to remind myself not to be fooled by the cry, 'What can one person do?' Hundreds of thousands of people down through the ages have proved that the actions of a single man or woman can change history.

Ask Rosa Parks, the formerly unnoticed black woman whose refusal to give up her bus seat to a white man gave impetus to the whole civil rights movement in America. Ask Laslo Tokes, the formerly unknown pastor responsible for being the catalyst of the Romanian revolution in 1989.

Who says one person can't make a difference? Try telling that to the victim of a landslide after one member of the public has just risked life and limb to rescue her from the suffocating debris. Tell it to an AIDS sufferer who has had a friend care for him in the last painful months of the disease.

'What can one person do?' Isn't that more often than not a cop-out, a lame-duck excuse for not getting involved in the pain of this world? Think about the fate of a starving child in Bangladesh if that child's sponsor decides to give up on sending his monthly gift.

Sure, each of us has real limitations. Yes, maybe some problems are so massive they're beyond us... when we're by ourselves. But what about those ordinary Filipinos who, in February 1986, stood in the way of the military on Manila's main highway, demonstrating to President Marcos that the people would no longer tolerate his corrupt rule? Tens of thousands of individuals each helped force the dictator to flee. Joined with others, we *can* make a difference.

True enough, in this life we will never deal with *all* the evil and suffering around us. But does that mean our efforts can't change one person's life... or one community? Sure, we can't tackle *every* problem. But there's no shortage of pain in the world. Each of us can help to ease some of it. If I believe that God intends goodness for his creatures, then even in the midst of great evil and suffering won't I be able to preserve *some* of that goodness? If we only ever help one person in our whole life, that will still be a miracle or a blessing for that one person.

And then let's never forget that small beginnings can sometimes produce vast and unexpected results. History is full of people whose first, tentative steps have led to huge changes – to a life that challenges the very source of suffering.

I've gathered together some examples of such people – as an encouragement to myself as well as to you. Here are five stories, the first amid the horrors of the Nazi terror; the second on the sand in the Roman Colosseum; the third in the slums of Calcutta; the fourth in the political scene at the height of the British Empire; and the fifth in the dark and silent world of a deaf girl.

Perhaps you and I will never make as much impact on our world as these people did. But if God's resurrection power rouses us to act in love, then we'll be following in the footsteps of Jesus. And if enough people do that, who knows where it will end?

★ ★ ★

Selected to starve – set free to live

The door of the bunker slammed shut. The ten naked, condemned men inside knew they would never emerge alive from their starvation cell. The taunt of the SS jailer rang in their ears: 'You will dry up like tulips.'

Nine of the men were selected to die by the brutal camp commandant, punished for the successful escape of a fellow inmate. Nine had been selected – the tenth had volunteered!

His name: Maximilian Kolbe. Age: 45. Occupation: monk. Nationality: Polish.

It was a death that other Auschwitz prisoners dreaded – a lingering agony without a drop of water or a crumb of food. There had been no need for Maximilian Kolbe to offer himself for such a death. But he did. Not as a way out of the horrors of the camp, not as an escape from the terror which stalked every prisoner's life (there were easier ways of ending it all) but to save the life of another.

It was mid-1941 and the tide of war was running the Germans' way. In the evil web of Nazi concentration camps, the violent treatment of inmates became ever more barbarous as the machinery of mass murder was refined. When a prisoner escaped, a system of collective responsibility was enforced. As punishment, men living in the same block were picked out to die in a starvation bunker.

Under the heat on a sultry day at the end of July, men from Barracks 14 – Father Kolbe's block – stood on the camp street all day tortured by sun, hunger (their last 'meal' had been the previous evening) and fear. A prisoner had escaped from a farming detail and they knew what to expect.

It was said that men condemned to the starvation bunker didn't even look like human beings after a day or two. With no liquid, their throats became raspy paper, their brains turned to fire and their intestines dried up, shrivelled like desiccated worms.

Barracks 14 waited, waited, waited for the inevitable sentences. Finally, at about seven o'clock in the evening, they came. Deputy Camp Commander Karl Fritsch and his assistant Gerhard Palitsch inspected the silent and exhausted rows of emaciated figures, and began selecting victims for the reprisal deaths.

One of the prisoners chosen shouted out in despair, 'My poor wife and children!' He was Franciszek Gajowniczek, a Polish sergeant.

Suddenly a frail figure, his eyes sunken behind round glasses with wire frames, his face flushed, his cheeks hollow, stepped out of line, took off his cap and moved with halting gait to stand at attention before the SS men.

Prisoners craned to see. Although desperate cries were not uncommon, no one had ever dared to break rank. It was probably this that kept Kolbe from being shot where he stood. His action was incomprehensible.

Fritsch, who had never before had any conversation with a prisoner, asked, 'What does this Polish pig want? Who are you?'

Kolbe replied, 'I am a Catholic priest. I want to die for that man; I am old; he has a wife and children.' It was a shrewd answer tailored to the Germans' philosophy of eliminating as priority the old and the weak.

Fritsch signalled Sergeant Gajowniczek to return to his place in the line and Palitsch, without a sign of emotion, changed the prisoner number on his death list.

Kolbe was led away, supporting one of the other men marked to die. Later, Gajowniczek said: 'I could only thank him with my eyes. I was stunned and could hardly grasp what was going on. The immensity of it: I, the condemned, am to live and someone else willingly and voluntarily offers his life for me – a stranger. Is this some dream, or reality?'

The other prisoners thanked God it wasn't them being led off to this drawn-out death. But after the shock of their own survival, the realisation of Kolbe's sacrifice began to sink in.

Another prisoner recalled: 'It was on everyone's lips, not just Poles. Czechs, Austrians, people of all nationalities – even the Germans – were dumbfounded and exclaimed, "This is genuine love of neighbour!" because no one had ever volunteered to die before. On the contrary, everyone held onto life to its last threads – and here Father Maximilian gave away, not a piece of his bread or even all his soup, but his very life for another. And such a death. In starvation like that, one has to give oneself up bit by bit, web by web, knowing for sure that one is perishing... To do it and not break down completely... '

Far from breaking down, Kolbe's faith made the death cell a place of hope and triumph over the inhuman brutality of the prison regime.

The condemned men were in a cell with a cement floor, completely devoid of furniture except for a bucket for relieving themselves. The extent of their suffering can be imagined from the fact that the urine bucket was always dry. In their horrifying, all-consuming thirst, the prisoners drank its contents. The foul air was horrible. They were in a frenzy, knowing that they would never return to their homes and families. They were screaming in despair and cursing. Until Father Kolbe pacified them. He prayed aloud, so they could join him. His voice could be heard in nearby cells, where other victims joined in.

'From then on, every day one heard the recitation of prayers, the rosary and hymns. Father Kolbe led while the others responded as a group.

'As these fervent prayers and hymns resounded in all corners of the bunker, I had the impression I was in a church... Sometimes Father Kolbe's group was so deeply absorbed in prayer that they didn't notice the SS opening the door... '

Father Kolbe never asked for anything and never complained. He looked directly and intently into the eyes of those entering the cell. The SS men couldn't stand his glance and used to yell at him, 'Shau auf die Erde, nicht auf uns!' ('Look at the ground, not at us!') Despite themselves, they admired his courage and behaviour.

(Originally published in my book *The Man Who Split History* and written for me by Chris Galloway.)

* * *

Sent by God – a lone voice

Telemachus had never been to Rome before. In fact, in his whole life he had probably travelled no more than 50 miles from his home. He was a hermit, devoted to a life of prayer and self-denial. So it was a scary thought when he sensed God saying to him one day, 'I want you to go to Rome.' Rome, the heart of the empire, the busiest, wealthiest city in the world. Though he was terrified at the prospect, Telemachus obeyed.

After weeks of journeying on foot over dusty roads, he finally arrived to find Rome in celebration mood. It was the early fifth century and the barbarian forces that threatened to overrun what remained of the empire had just been defeated. Alaric the Goth, who had sacked Rome, was now dead and peace seemed assured.

Looking for clues as to why God wanted him in Rome, Telemachus followed the crowds to the Colosseum. He had no idea where they were going or what he would find there, but taking a seat in that huge stadium he could hear the roar of wild animals that seemed to come from below.

Suddenly men dressed for battle poured into the centre of the stadium. They faced the emperor, and shouted 'We who are about to die, salute thee'. Telemachus felt a chill go up his spine. Even though he still had little idea of what was about to happen, instinctively he knew it was not good.

Gladiatorial games had long been one of the main forms of entertainment for the Roman population. For centuries the empire had been in decay. No surer sign than this – the sight of men killing each other in front of amused crowds.

As the 'games' began, Telemachus felt a sickening knot in his gut. The moral outrage was too much. Rising from his seat to leave, he was suddenly gripped by the conviction that he couldn't, indeed he shouldn't, just walk away. He must do something.

Without thinking, the country monk hopped up to the top of the perimeter wall and shouted out, 'In the name of Christ, stop this!' Not surprisingly no one even blinked an eyelid at his ridiculous posturing. So Telemachus jumped into the arena. Running out into the middle he attempted to get between two gladiators. As if to try and reason with them he shouted, 'Stop! This is madness. In the name of Christ, please stop!' One of the warriors pushed him aside with his shield. He fell, sprawling on the sand. A small monk was no match for powerfully built warriors.

Telemachus scrambled to his feet. Without thought for his safety he rushed at another couple of gladiators locked in battle, imploring them, begging them to stop. The crowd roared. Thinking that he was part of the entertainment for the day, they began to laugh and cheer.

Telemachus kept on trying to stop the gladiators. 'In the name of Christ, stop!' he shouted, again and again. But with more than their opponents to watch, a couple of the fighters soon began to get angry at the little fellow.

Sensing their frustration, the crowd turned on Telemachus. The joke was finished. He was becoming a distraction to their fun. 'Run him through!' a couple of spectators yelled. 'Slice him in half!'

Within seconds one of the gladiators did just that. In one swift, easy motion a sword flashed across Telemachus's stomach. Blood spewed out and the monk slumped to the ground, gasping one more time, 'In the name of Christ, stop!'

The stadium fell strangely silent. From the top of the Colosseum one person stood up and walked out. He was followed by another, and then another. Soon people were leaving in droves. It was not long before the whole stadium was virtually emptied.

Reputedly, that was the last gladiatorial contest in the Roman Colosseum. No doubt other things contributed, but the small monk's foolhardy and almost naive action was the trigger that eventually brought the madness to an end.

(My source for this story is Charles Colson's *Loving God*, Zondervan 1983, a great book which contains a number of true stories of people who've gone out on a limb to express their commitment to Christ.)

* * *

The Angel of Calcutta

In 1929 eighteen-year-old Agnes Bojaxhiv left her comfortable home in Yugoslavia, bound for the shores of India. Life had been good to her. Coming from a wealthy Albanian family, she had had everything she needed. Yet Agnes sensed God calling her to serve him in the East.

For 18 years she worked as a geography teacher in a school for girls in Calcutta. She took her final vows as a nun in 1937. As time passed she became more and more dismayed by the dreadful living conditions in the city. She was shocked by the thousands of people who lived and died on the streets. Walking through Calcutta she agonised over the utter desperation in their eyes – a silent, endless pleading for help.

It wasn't long before Agnes realised God was telling her to look after some of these people. While the call was clear to her, it was not so obvious to her superiors. It was no easy task to convince them that she should stop teaching and begin a new work in the inner city. The nun's health was frail and her abilities were limited. Even she agreed that there was nothing special about her, save a deep and strong friendship with Jesus.

Finally, after years of requests, she was granted permission to start her new work. She had no money and no helpers. But the adventure had begun.

Her first patient was a man from the gutter, infested with worms and smelling unbearably foul. Lifting him up, she wiped his decaying body and washed his wounds.

'Why are you doing this?' he asked weakly.

With tenderness and compassion, she whispered back, 'Because I love you.'

As she began to care for the very worst of the poor, the gentle nun treated each person as if this was Jesus himself. Dignity and worth were restored to many, even in death.

For nearly 50 years Mother Teresa walked the streets of Calcutta showing the love of Jesus in word and in action. Her example led thousands of others to discover also the strange joy and fulfilment that comes from serving the poor. Not just in Calcutta, but in cities around the world.

Even well into her eighties, Mother Teresa shunned luxury and money. The pain she felt as she served the untouchables of Calcutta remained the same. When finally she died her name had become a household word – convincing even our modern sceptical world that one person *can* make a difference.

The conscience of England

Two young men walked into the House of Commons and took their seats. It was clear they were a little nervous. Barely out of Cambridge and just 21, William Pitt and William Wilberforce sensed the significance of the occasion. Both were new MPs and they looked forward to a long career in the British Parliament. The year was 1780 and England was in crisis as a result of a revolt in the American colonies.

It was not long before the two friends' careers began to move in different directions. Within 20 months of arriving in Parliament, William Pitt the Younger was Chancellor of the Exchequer and by the age of 24 he was Prime Minister. He would become one of the great British prime ministers, serving (with short gaps) in that capacity until his death in 1806.

Wilberforce, the more ambitious of the two, was also on the brink of a highly distinguished career. He quickly became one of the greatest orators in the House, and carried with him a charisma that enabled him to remain independent, rising above party politics. But not long after his friend had moved to Downing Street, Wilberforce embarked on an extended holiday abroad with an older friend. When he returned to England, the change in Wilberforce was remarkable. He had undergone a profound spiritual conversion to Christianity and it soon began to impact on his thoughts about the future.

Tempted to give up the political life, William Wilberforce was convinced by John Newton to stay, and to use his considerable skills and charisma for good. Newton (writer of the classic hymn *Amazing Grace*) had been captain of a slave trader for years, until his own remarkable conversion. As he began to unfold to Wilberforce the horrors of the Atlantic slave trade, the young politician soon saw a cause that was worth fighting for.

By 1787 Wilberforce had joined with a number of others in an attempt to have the slave trade abolished. Since many of the group lived in the small village of Clapham, just outside London, they came to be known as the Clapham Sect. Wilberforce and his friends knew the task would not be easy. The slave trade had been operating since the sixteenth century and was the largest enforced migration in history.

But more than that, it had become critical to the British economy – as it also had on the Continent. Ships, laden with cheap goods, alcohol and arms, left the ports of England and

Europe, bound for west Africa. There the cargoes were traded for newly acquired black African slaves. Chained in horrific conditions, the slaves were then transported across the Atlantic to the West Indies and America, unloaded and sold. Many slaves never made it that far, dying on the way. Finally the ships, reloaded with sugar, rum and cotton, returned to Europe. It was a trade that brought handsome profits.

The powerful, vested interests who pocketed those profits were well represented in the English Parliament. More than that, many Britons saw the trade as an economic necessity. Wilberforce and his friends knew it would be a huge undertaking to fight these interests. Not only did they try, time and time again, to introduce bills to Parliament, but they publicised the tragic stories of slaves, and mobilised public opinion in a way that had never previously been attempted.

For 20 long years the campaign continued until finally, on 23 February, 1807, the House of Commons voted for abolition. The 'great evil' had, at least legally, come to an end. However, for years an illicit trade operated, though much reduced in power. For this reason the Clapham Sect embarked on a further campaign – this time to have slavery abolished in the British Empire.

Finally, in 1833, 46 years after starting out, William Wilberforce, now on his death bed, heard the news that Parliament had voted to free all slaves in the Empire. He died a few days later.

Wilberforce was a brilliant orator and could have held high office like his friend Pitt. Yet, his influence was greater than any other single person of his day. Laying ambition aside, he sought to fight for a number of causes. The result – an end to the suffering of hundreds of thousands of people across the globe.

★　★　★

Dedicated to alleviate suffering

Almost everyone has heard of Helen Keller. Her story has been told the world round. Born in 1880 in Alabama, USA, Helen lost her sight and hearing at 19 months, as a result of an unknown disease. Soon after, unable to communicate, she also lost the power of speech. For five years Helen plunged into a terrifying life of loneliness. She later described herself as 'a Phantom living in a world that was no-world'.

When she was six years old Helen's parents took her to Baltimore to see a famous oculist, who then referred them on to Alexander Graham Bell. Although Helen's disabilities presented huge obstacles to learning, Bell was optimistic and told the Kellers about the Perkins Institution for the Blind. As a result the director sent a 21-year-old graduate down to Alabama, with the aim of trying to teach Helen.

The young graduate's name was Annie Sullivan and no one, including Annie, expected much. The chances of teaching deaf/blind children anything were very slim. Annie herself, had endured much in her short life. The daughter of Irish immigrants, she was born into dreadful poverty. Her mother died when she was eight and her father abandoned all three children two years later. No one wanted Annie – who was half-blind herself – and her younger brother, so they were sent to the state infirmary, which was no more than an almshouse. Conditions at the orphanage were by all accounts abysmal. Annie's brother Jimmie died within a few years. Disease and degradation were rampant, so bad in fact that a state inquiry into the place was ordered.

Told by one of her orphan friends that there were special schools for the blind, Annie took the opportunity during the inquiry to plead her case. Mercifully, she was sent to the Perkins Institution, aged 14, and began learning to read with her fingers. During the time she was there both her eyes were operated on with some limited success. She was able to read for short periods of time, but not well enough for her to be educated at a normal school. She graduated from Perkins in 1886, and was offered the chance to teach the Keller girl.

Annie arrived in Alabama on 3 March, 1887, a date that Helen later described as her 'soul's birthday'. Annie at once began spelling words in Helen's hand. A month later Helen connected with what her teacher was doing. While Annie Sullivan pumped water over her hand, Helen realised that the finger motions she had just felt on her palm meant water. 'In that thrilling moment,' says one biographer, 'she found the key to her kingdom. Everything had a name and she had a way to learn the names.'

This was the beginning of a wonderful adventure for Helen. With Annie Sullivan at her side, she learnt all manner of things. Her progress was rapid and at the age of 10 Helen announced she was going to learn to talk with her mouth like other people and not by use of her fingers. Though she never mastered the art completely, Helen quickly achieved an understandable gutteral speech. Her first words in English were, 'I am not dumb now'.

Helen and 'Teacher' were always together, and at the age of 20 (in 1900) Helen entered Radcliffe College, graduating four years later with a degree. Annie married a literary critic and they all lived in Wrentham, Massachusetts.

Helen began to write. One of her early books, *The Story of My Life*, became a classic and was continuously in print for more than 50 years. She wrote about social issues too – such as women's suffrage and socialism. They went on lecture tours, did a movie on her life (which was a box office flop) and even performed an act in live theatre. Most times they were on the edge of poverty.

In 1923 Helen joined the American Foundation for the Blind and began campaigning for them. By the 1930s Annie's sight was gone and she finally died on 20 October, 1936.

For the rest of her life Helen travelled the world speaking on behalf of the blind and other disabled groups, inspiring audiences and helping develop rehabilitation programmes. 'Alone we can do so little,' she insisted. 'Together we can do so much.'

Both women spent their lives dedicated to a cause. Annie discovered through her wonderful gift of teaching the great joy that one person could gain from being able to communicate with the outside world. She sacrificed much in order to give Helen the help and friendship she desperately needed. Helen always felt that the plaudits and honours awarded to her should have been awarded to her teacher. Even after Annie's death Helen would say, 'People think Teacher has left me, but she is with me all the time.'

Helen's cause was a life-long commitment to alleviate the suffering of others. She looked on herself as a humble instrument in the hands of God, 'gripped by the might of the destiny she (Annie) had mapped out for me; it lifted me out of myself to wage God's war against darkness.'

12: Making sense of the senseless

It may be hard – impossible even – to see a reason for suffering. Throughout history, men and women have acted on their belief that suffering is wrong and should be opposed. Some have chosen lifelong careers to remove its causes – like Dr Paul Brand. Some have led resistance against injustice – like Martin Luther King. Some have battled in their own lives to overcome the disability that has afflicted them – like Helen Keller. Sometimes they have endured year after year before meeting success – like William Wilberforce and Mother Teresa. Sometimes they have died seeing no change to the evil they stood against – like Telemachus or Maximilian Kolbe.

But regardless of success or change, they believed that God called them to resist. To share with him in shouldering the burden of this battered world. Is it an accident that so many stories of compassion in the midst of suffering involve men and women with a deep faith? There are many reasons why Christians are willing to endure so much for others, but an important part of the explanation is, so to speak, out of this world...

The future with God

The life, death and resurrection of Jesus is, I believe, proof that God can be trusted. While he was here on this earth, Jesus made it clear that eventually justice would be done. In the end, good will prevail. At the close of this world God will make things right.

Ultimately, the answer to the question of pain and suffering comes down to an issue of trust. Can we trust God? I believe we can.

Is there a purpose and meaning in suffering? There is – because God chose to endure it himself. Is there a part we can play in preventing wrongs and injustice? There is – because God asks us to follow in the footsteps of his Son. More than that, when it comes to the crunch, the moment of commitment, the point where we take the plunge and follow in the path that Jesus trod before us... an unexpected miracle takes place. Jesus is there with us. We're not on our own. We're not relying on just our own weak strength. God is providing us, somehow, with extra resources to do what he's called us to do.

So, though we don't know the whole answer, we do know that there *is* one. Though we don't know the whole explanation, we can see enough of it to trust that God is indeed in control.

God cares about our pain. He too has experienced suffering. Through that suffering, his plan to end all injustice is already in action. And we have a part to play in it. Even now, here in this fractured world, our own pain can bring us, and others, closer to God.

* * *

Thursday, one year after my brother's death

A whole year since Phil died. Those few days of that fateful February are still etched in my memory. It's all so close to the surface that the smallest and silliest things trigger the same feelings. Will it always be like this? How long will the emotional nerves remain raw and exposed? Will they ever be dulled?

It seems that I'm not going to be allowed to forget. Believe it or not, on this day – the anniversary of Phil's death – I'm back in church for another funeral service. This time it's for a friend's mother who has died of cancer. She was someone Phil knew really well.

I have some inkling of the desolation her family must be experiencing at this moment. I feel awkward, moved deeply by the service and my memories of the woman, yet strangely removed. I feel like a voyeur of grief at work.

After the service, I spend some time at Phil's graveside, just thinking.

Final reflections

There will be more pain to face in future years, I'm sure about that. How will I cope? I honestly don't know. How does anybody?

The words of Craig's poem, penned the day after Phil died, remind me of my brother:

Unique as the sunset woven on summer horizons

Phil you flamed our lives with golden laughter,

poured generous seed upon hungry soil,

smiled honestly around a cut-throat world.

Good memories; not-so-good memories. But in the midst of it all there's the hope of a new tomorrow... when all that now is will be gone... when God will right all wrongs... for eternity.

Is there really a future for us? Am I a fool to believe that all this pain and suffering the world is going through is only temporary? I do believe it. Such a belief puts all my own suffering into perspective this day. Not that I understand any more of it. Just that I have someone to trust through the turmoil and pain.

He knows. He understands. He cares. And ultimately he will make all right.

If you want to read more...

More titles in this same subject area of facing up to pain and suffering, published by SCRIPTURE UNION:

Sweet Tales from the Bitter Edge by **Gethin Russell-Jones**
Graphic and honest stories of people on the edge, struggling to make sense of extreme circumstances, and trying to press on to know God.

Skeletons in Messiah's Cupboard by **Gethin Russell-Jones**
A book about coping with family skeletons, imaginatively describing a range of family nightmares everyday and unusual, and the hope there is in belonging to God and his family.

Encounter with God in Job by **Dennis Lennon**
What is God's involvement in the painful moments of life? This book explores the powerful themes that arise from Job's distressing predicament.

The Courage to Hope by **Peter Sampson**
Practical help for Christians facing bereavement, and for those caring for them.

How to Pray When Life Hurts by **Roy Lawrence**
Whether we feel guilty or angry, fearful or under pressure, this book offers practical help on how to pray.

Children and Grieving by **Janet Goodall**
Written for anyone helping children through the pain of bereavement.

Hope in Despair by **Des Summerson**
Six studies exploring how God views the poor and oppressed; a book which challenges our response to a world where so many live in poverty.

SU books are available from your local Christian bookshop or by mail order: Scripture Union (Mail Order), PO Box 5148, Milton Keynes MLO, MK2 2YX. Telephone 01908 856006. Fax 01908 856020.

And by other publishers:
Where Is God When It Hurts? by **Philip Yancey** (Zondervan, Grand Rapids, 1977)
Disappointment With God by **Philip Yancey** (HarperCollins, New York, 1988)
Joni by **Joni Eareckson-Tada** (Zondervan)
The Hiding Place by **Corrie ten Boom** (Hodder & Stoughton, London, 1971)
The Man Who Split History by **Wayne Kirkland** (Signpost Communications, 1995, PO Box 7057, Wellington, New Zealand)